Toccatas, Carillons and Scherzos for Organ

27 Works
for Church or Concert Performance

Selected and Edited by
ROLLIN SMITH

DOVER PUBLICATIONS, INC.
Mineola, New York

Copyright

Copyright © 2002 by Dover Publications, Inc.
All rights reserved.

Bibliographical Note

This Dover edition, first published in 2002, is a new compilation of works originally published separately in authoritative early editions along with others that have been newly edited and engraved by Rollin Smith for this volume. His Notes on the Music were prepared specially for this publication.

International Standard Book Number
ISBN-13: 978-0-486-42431-6
ISBN-10: 0-486-42431-6

Manufactured in the United States by RR Donnelley
42431607   2015
www.doverpublications.com

CONTENTS

Notes on the Music iv

TOCCATAS

Bach, Johann Sebastian	Toccata and Fugue in D minor (BWV 565) *(ed. Lemare)*	**2**
Boëllmann, Léon	Toccata (from *Suite gothique,* Op. 25)	**16**
Callaerts, Joseph	Toccata in E minor	**26**
Dubois, Théodore	Toccata in G major (from *Douze Pièces*)	**33**
Fletcher, Percy E.	Festival Toccata	**45**
Gigout, Eugène	Toccata in B minor (from *Dix Pièces*)	**62**
MacMaster, Georges	Toccata in A major (Op. 67, No. 2)	**71**
Mailly, Alphonse	Toccata in D minor (from *Trois Pièces*)	**78**
Mulet, Henri	"Tu es petra" (Toccata) (from *Esquisses Byzantines*)	**85**
Renaud, Albert	Toccata in D minor (Op. 108, No. 1)	**96**
Renzi, Remigio	Toccata in E major	**105**
Shelley, Harry Rowe	Fanfare d'Orgue	**115**
Tournemire, Charles	Toccata in B minor (from *Suite de Morceaux,* Op. 19)	**123**
Widor, Charles-Marie	Toccata (from Symphony V, Op. 42, No. 1)	**130**
Yon, Pietro A.	Humoresque, "L'Organo Primitivo"	**140**

CARILLONS

Boëllmann, Léon	Carillon (from *Douze Pièces,* Op. 16)	**148**
Bourdon, Émile	Carillons (from *Dix Pièces,* Op. 7)	**153**
Grison, Jules	Les Cloches: Verset-Prelude for the *Magnificat*	**159**
Marty, Adolphe	Les Carillons de Saint-Paul d'Orléans	**166**
Morandi, Giovanni	Rondò con imitazione de' campanelli (Bell Rondo, Op. 17)	**173**
Mulet, Henri	Carillon–Sortie in D major	**179**
Sowerby, Leo	Carillon	**189**

SCHERZOS

Bingham, Seth	Roulade (from *Six Pieces,* Op. 9)	**196**
Bossi, Marco Enrico	Scherzo in G minor (Op. 49, No. 2)	**207**
Dethier, Gaston M.	Scherzo	**218**
Fumagalli, Polibio	Capriccio, "La Caccia" (Op. 257)	**230**
Gigout, Eugène	Scherzo in E major (from *Dix Pièces*)	**236**

Notes on the Music

Most friends have been won for the organ by having heard an organist play a brilliant toccata, carillon, or scherzo. This collection offers a variety of these attractive church and concert works—many available for the first time since their original publication—in a mix of virtuoso organ works and less technically demanding pieces guaranteed to produce a brilliant effect. In addition to French, English, Belgian, German, and American music that spans more than 250 years, this edition includes five pieces by Italian composers of the Romantic era.

TOCCATAS

Bach: Toccata and Fugue in D minor (BWV 565)

This is a facsimile of the edition prepared in 1911 by the great Edwin H. Lemare. He stated in his preface that, while not approving of "constant change of manuals and grotesque stop combinations," nevertheless "the evolution of the organ has resulted in such tonal and mechanical improvements that it is possible, I think, to revive much of the waning interest, on the part of the general public, in these masterpieces, by a more 'life-like' rendering and, in many cases, by an increased tempo . . . ."

"The points, in this edition, which I have kept chiefly in mind, are:

1st. Careful and natural phrasing of both manual and pedal part.

2nd. Clearness of engraving in the more intricate parts.

3rd Division of the two hands, as much as possible, into the two staves.

4th. Careful marking of the Pedal part to induce freedom of action and increased speed.

5th. Full stop registration, in accordance with the organ of the present day.

"It may be that—for the sake of clearness of reading—in dividing the hands into the two staves, I have somewhat disturbed the continuity of the parts as seen and followed on paper. But my object has been to render the arrangement easy for the player; rather than present an edition for the study, in cold hard type, of the wonderful counterpoint and fugal development contained in Bach's works.

"Unnecessary rests—from the player's point of view— have therefore been eliminated, and the one great object— *viz:* the effect of performance—is my excuse for offering this edition."

Boëllmann: Toccata (from *Suite gothique,* Op. 25)

Born in the Alsatian village of Ensisheim in 1862, Léon Boëllmann entered the École Niedermeyer in Paris in 1874. Studying with Clément Loret and Eugène Gigout, he won first prize in all his subjects and, at the age of 19, was appointed *organiste du chœur* at the church of Saint-Vincent-de-Paul— apparently the only church with which he was associated; on the death of Henri Fissot, in 1896, Boëllmann succeeded him as *titulaire*. He was a brilliant organist and a fine composer, especially of chamber music, but his life was cut short by illness at the age of 35.

Although Boëllmann left 68 published works, only his *Variations symphoniques* for cello and orchestra—first played at the Concerts Lamoureaux in 1892—and the *Suite gothique* for organ (1895) have become repertory standards. The latter, his most famous work, was dedicated to the American organist William C. Carl.

Callaerts: Toccata in E minor

Born in Antwerp, Joseph-Jacques Callaerts studied at the Brussels Conservatoire with Jacques-Nicolas Lemmens and subsequently became organist of Antwerp Cathedral. In 1876 he was appointed professor of organ at Peter Benoit's Flemish Music School. Jan Blockx was one of Callaerts' most famous students.

Dubois: Toccata in G major (from *Douze Pièces*)

This Toccata—the most popular of Théodore Dubois' 88 organ works—was dedicated to Alphonse Mailly. Dubois succeeded Saint-Saëns as organist of La Madeleine in 1877, and taught harmony and composition at the Paris Conservatoire, succeeding Ambroise Thomas as director in 1896.

Fletcher: Festival Toccata

A native of Derby, England, Percy Fletcher went to London at the age of 20 and pursued a career as musical director at various theaters, including His Majesty's Theatre, where he conducted for the last 17 years of his life. The *Festival Toccata* dates from 1915 and has long been popular, owing to both its overall appeal and technical facility.

Gigout: Toccata in B minor (from *Dix Pièces*)

During the late 1860s, the young Eugène Gigout was Gabriel Fauré's classmate at Paris' École Niedermeyer where both studied piano with Saint-Saëns. At 19, Gigout was appointed organist of the new church of Saint-Augustin where he remained for the next 57 years. He established his own organ school, teaching there until 1911; he then succeeded Alexandre Guilmant as Paris Conservatoire's professor of organ. Saint-Saëns considered Gigout the greatest organist he had ever known.

This Toccata was published in 1892 in a collection of *Dix Pièces* and was dedicated to the famous American organist Clarence Eddy. French musicologist Norbert Dufourcq wrote that "Cleverness is not enough to write such music; Gigout was not only a wizard with notes, but a Latin genius concerned with balance, proportion, and clarity." The composer recorded the Toccata in 1912 on a Welte player organ roll, at a the tempo of ♩ = 116.

MacMaster: Toccata in A major (Op. 67, No. 2)

The expatriate Englishman Georges MacMaster studied in Paris and founded the Institut MacMaster—a school in which 14 professors taught music, painting, and declamation. He was organist of Saint-Ambroise (1874–90), and later of the Église Wesleyenne (1890–98). MacMaster took his own life on 31 March 1898—in the words of his obituary in *Le Monde Musical: "a mis fin brusquement à ses jours."*

Mailly: Toccata in D minor (from *Trois Pièces*)

Alphonse-Jean-Ernest Mailly studied with Lemmens and was his successor as professor of organ at the Brussels Conservatoire, a post he held from 1869 until 1903. His most famous student was Charles Courboin, former organist of St. Patrick's Cathedral, New York. Considered to be the finest organist in Belgium, and praised by Hector Berlioz, Mailly held the title *Organiste du Roi*. He played several times in Paris, notably in 1858 at the inauguration of the Cavaillé-Coll organ in the Church of Saint-Vincent-de-Paul and, in 1878, at the Trocadéro's inaugural organ recital series. This Toccata, the third of *Trois Pièces,* has a right-hand figuration similar to that of Widor's Toccata, and a left-hand theme reminiscent of Mendelssohn's *Fingal's Cave Overture.*

Mulet: "Tu es petra" (Toccata)

Henri Mulet's brilliant piece closes his *Esquisses Byzantines*—ten movements "en mémoire de la Basilique du Sacré-Cœur de Montmartre 1914–1919"—the church built as a monument of repentance for France's defeat in the Franco-Prussian War. The title of Mullet's music—"Tu es petra et portæ inferi non prævalebunt adversus te"—refers to Jesus' play-on-words addressed to his apostle Peter: "Thou art the rock and upon this rock I will build my church."

Renaud: Toccata in D minor (Op. 108, No. 1)

After studies with Delibes and Franck at the Paris Conservatoire, Albert Renaud succeeeded his father as maître-de-chapelle of Saint-Sulpice. Following a brief period as organist of the Cathedral of Rennes, he assumed the post at Paris' Saint-François-Xavier (1879–91) and finally at Saint-Germain-en-Laye. This Toccata is dedicated to Alexandre Guilmant, who performed it at the St. Louis World's Fair in 1904.

Renzi: Toccata in E major

The brilliant Roman organist Remigio Renzi was professor of organ at the Santa Cecilia Academy—numbering Pietro Yon among his students—and organist of the Vatican from 1883 until his death in 1938.

Shelley: Fanfare d'Orgue

In the years that spanned the 19th and 20th centuries, Harry Rowe Shelley—famous for his anthem "Hark! Hark! My Soul"—was one of only two or three eminent American church music composers. He had been Charles Ives's composition teacher, and the manuscript of Ives's *Variations on "America"* bears his corrections. In 1904, when Shelley wrote this "étude de concert," he was organist of the Fifth Avenue Baptist Church in New York. When he told a group of friends that he had written this "Fanfare," Shelley was reminded that Lemmens had already written one. "Mine's different," he replied.

Tournemire: Toccata in B minor (Op. 19, N0. 3)

This is the third movement of the *Suite de morceaux pour Grand Orgue,* Op. 19, published in 1900 and dedicated to Ferdinand de la Tombelle. Charles Tournemire had been a student of Franck and Widor at the Paris Conservatoire, and succeeded Gabriel Pierné as organist of Sainte-Clotilde in Paris. Although most of his organ music is based on themes derived from Gregorian chant, this early Toccata demonstrates his concept of "orchestration" for the organ, involving tessitura and texture as well as imaginative registration.

Widor: Toccata (from *Organ Symphony V*)

Charles-Marie Widor became organist of Saint-Sulpice in 1870, shortly before his 26th birthday, and within nine years composed—among other works—his first six organ symphonies. He premiered his Fifth Symphony, Op. 42, No. 1, in a recital at the Trocadéro in October 1879. The Toccata that serves as the symphony's finale is, as its name implies, a "touch piece"—one of the very first "perpetual motions" written for the organ, featuring arpeggiated *ostinato* figurations above the repeated martial chords. Norbert Dufourcq wrote: "There is not one piece in French organ music that flies more directly to the heart of the audience than the *Toccata in F."*

Following its publication in 1879, Widor's organ symphony was revised four times. In 1887, the metronome marking ♩ = 118 was added to the Toccata; in 1900–1, accents were added to the left-hand chords; in 1927, the metronome was reduced to ♩ = 100, with slurs added over the first two sixteenths of each right-hand figuration.

Yon: Humoresque, "L'Organo Primitivo"

A native of the Piedmont region of Italy, Pietro Yon studied with Fumagalli, Remondi, Renzi, Bolzoni, and Sgambati. He immigrated to America in 1907 and succeeded Gaston Dethier as organist of St. Francis Xavier Church in New York. In 1927, he was appointed organist of St. Patrick's Cathedral and—with the most famous Catholic church in America as his base—wielded great influence over Catholic church music.

Subtitled "Toccatina for Flute," Yon's *Humoresque for a Primitive Organ* (1918) was inspired by the sight of an ancient instrument in New York's Metropolitan Museum of Art. Dedicated to noted organist and teacher Clarence Dickinson, the music was intended to be played on a single eight-foot flute stop.

CARILLONS

Boëllmann: Carillon (from *Douze Pièces,* Op. 16)

The famous Carillon from Bizet's *L'Arlésienne Suite No. 1* influenced at least two organ composers. The three-note bell motive G♯–E–F♯—repeated for 52 measures—was first imitated, in inversion and a half-step higher (F–A–G)—by Théodore Dubois throughout an *Entrée en forme de Carillon*

(1889), and the next year by Léon Boëllmann in the fifth of his *Douze Pièces,* Op. 16, dedicated to Dubois. Boëllmann's music explores the motive in D major: D–F♯–E.

Bourdon: Carillons (from *Dix Pièces,* Op. 7)

Marcel Dupré and Émile Bourdon were fellow students in Guilmant's organ class at the Paris Conservatoire. Later, when Bourdon was organist of the Cathedral of Monaco, he published his *Dix Pièces,* Op. 7. "Carillons"—the second piece of the set—was dedicated to Dupré. In turn—as a tribute to his old friend—Dupré included this new work on recitals, and chose it as the first piece he was ever to record: a player organ roll for the Aeolian Company.

Grison:
Les Cloches: Verset–Prelude for the *Magnificat*

In Catholic liturgy, the Feast of All Saints (November 1) is followed by the Feast of All Souls (November 2). The first is a festival day of rejoicing, honoring all the saints; the second, a solemn commemoration of the departed. The afternoon service of Vespers for the Feast of All Saints is followed by Vespers for the Dead.

For centuries it was the custom in France to toll a funeral bell announcing the office of the dead during the *Magnificat,* the last canticle sung at the first service.

This coincidence of festival, funeral, and the ringing of bells has inspired composers to flavor their improvised *versets* (instrumental interludes alternating with sung verses) with bell effects as well as with quotations from the *Dies irae*—the sequence from the Gregorian Requiem—the Mass said on All Souls Day.

Jules Grison was a student of the organist of Reims Cathedral, succeeding him at age 21. Grison's *Les Cloches* (1890)—subtitled "The Mournful Bells of Reims"—is a six-movement suite of preludes, or *versets,* dedicated to the memory of the composer's father.

In this—the sixth and final *verset* of the set—thunder is introduced at the statement of the *Dies irae.* The thunder pedal—common on French organs before the 20th century—played several of the lowest pedal notes simultaneously, giving a fine imitation of the rumble of thunder.

Marty: Les Carillons de Saint-Paul d'Orléans

Afflicted since infancy, Adolphe Marty—a student of Franck—was the first blind student to win a first prize in organ at the Paris Conservatoire. From 1886 to 1888 he was organist of Saint-Paul in Orléans, then moved to Paris to teach at the Institution Nationale des Jeunes Aveugles (The National Institution for Blind Youth). Among his students were Louis Vierne, André Marchal, Jean Langlais, and Gaston Litaize.

Inspired by the carillon at Saint-Paul, Marty's "Les Carillons" is part of *L'Orgue triomphal*—a set of twelve organ pieces published in 1898. (Vierne performed this work on his 1927 transcontinental tour of North America.)

Explaining the source of his music, Marty wrote:

> The largest bell [at Saint-Paul] sounds D; in between strikes, the *carillonneur* rings embellishments on the three other bells, sounding the notes G–F–E. In the midst of ringing, the *carillonneur* pauses, leaving the biggest bell to sound alone, after which he begins again. This style of ringing has changed since 1897.

A unique facet of this music is the persistence of the pedal-note D until the next-to-last measure.

Morandi: Rondò con imitazione de' campanelli (Bell Rondo, Op. 17)

Percussion stops on organs are not new; indeed, they were not unknown on early Italian organs, and were, in effect, *glockenspiels* played by the organ action.

Choirmaster of the Cathedral in Senigalia, and composer of twelve books of organ sonatas, Giovanni Morandi integrated this instrumental effect into his "Bell Rondo," the most famous of his works. The intermittent pedal part has been retained as it appears in the original edition.

Mulet: Carillon–Sortie in D major

A pupil of Widor and Guilmant at the Paris Conservatoire, Henri Mulet won first prizes in cello and harmony, and second prize in organ. He taught at the École Niedermeyer and was organist of Saint-Philippe-du-Roule until 1937, when he retired from Paris, gave up composition, and moved to Provence. Mulet's two celebrated organ works are included in this volume: the Toccata "Tu es petra" and this *Carillon-Sortie*—one of the finest of modern Carillons.

Sowerby: Carillon

Leo Sowerby's piece is one of the most endearing and enduring American organ works. It is a tasteful vehicle for displaying the instrument's harp and chimes, two organ stops that remain high in popular appeal. Sowerby recorded this music in May 1946, on the organ of Chicago's Saint James' Cathedral. His tempo is ♩ = 88.

SCHERZOS

Bingham: Roulade (Op. 9, No. 3)

A student of Horatio Parker and Harry Benjamin Jepson at Yale, and of d'Indy, Widor, and Guilmant in Paris, Seth Bingham served on the music faculty of Columbia University for over 40 years and as organist and music director at New York's Madison Avenue Presbyterian Church for 35 years.

"Roulade," one of *Six Pieces,* Op. 9, was dedicated to David McK. Williams, then organist of New York's Saint Bartholomew's Church. It has remained the composer's most popular work.

Bossi: Scherzo in G minor (Op. 49, No. 2)

Following studies with Ponchielli and Fumagalli in Milan, Marco Enrico Bossi held successive appointments at conservatories in Naples, Venice, and Bologna (where he was Malipiero's composition teacher) before his appointment as director of Rome's celebrated Liceo Santa Cecilia. Bossi came to the United States in December 1924 for a series of recitals, but illness caused most of them to be canceled. He died in 1925, two days out to sea as he was returning home to Italy.

A brilliant organist, Bossi is considered perhaps modern Italy's finest organ composer. In this Scherzo in G minor—his most famous work—his austere writing is characterized by aggressive chords, full-organ climaxes, and more contrapuntal development than mere lateral melody. A sense of clever nuance and the facilities of the concert organ pervade his works.

Dethier: Scherzo

Belgian-born, Gaston-Marie Dethier left the Liège Conservatoire at 17 with first prizes in organ, harmony, and fugue. Two years later, on the recommendation of Alexandre Guilmant, he immigrated to America and became organist of New York's Saint Francis Xavier Church. A brilliant organist and celebrated composer, Dethier was also a founder of the American Guild of Organists. He was the first organ teacher at the Institute of Musical Arts (founded in 1905), and succeeded Carl Friedberg on the piano faculty. He continued to teach both instruments after the Institute became the Juilliard School of Music.

Fumagalli: Capriccio, "La Caccia" (Op. 257)

Polibio Fumagalli was the second youngest of four brothers from Inzago, Italy. While all were celebrated pianists and prolific composers, Polibio was the most productive with over 300 published works. "La Caccia" (The Hunt) was his most successful organ work, becoming a standard recital work well into the 20th century as a result of frequent performances by English virtuoso W. T. Best.

Choirmaster of Milan's Church of Saint Celso for over 20 years, Fumagalli also served as professor of organ at the Milan Conservatory. There, he taught both Marco Enrico Bossi and Pietro Yon—two celebrated organists represented in this collection.

Gigout: Scherzo in E major (from *Dix Pièces*)

Another of Gigout's *Ten Pieces* of 1892, this Scherzo is a delightful concert work from the late 19th century. Its calculated proportions are the essence of Gallic grace—an aspect of the music that requires elegance, suppleness, and subtle phrasing.

ROLLIN SMITH
Spring 2002

TOCCATAS

TOCCATA AND FUGUE IN D MINOR

IV Solo (Reeds *fff*)
III Swell (Full)
II Great (Diapasons 16' & 8') — III
I Choir (Full)
Pedal (Full - without Reeds) — II & III

Johann Sebastian Bach
1685–1750

Edited by Edwin H. Lemare

8 / Bach

10 / Bach

12 / Bach

14 / Bach

TOCCATA

from *Suite Gothique*, Op. 25

Léon Boëllmann
1862–1897

Boëllmann / 17

18 / *Boëllmann*

Boëllmann / 21

22 / Boëllmann

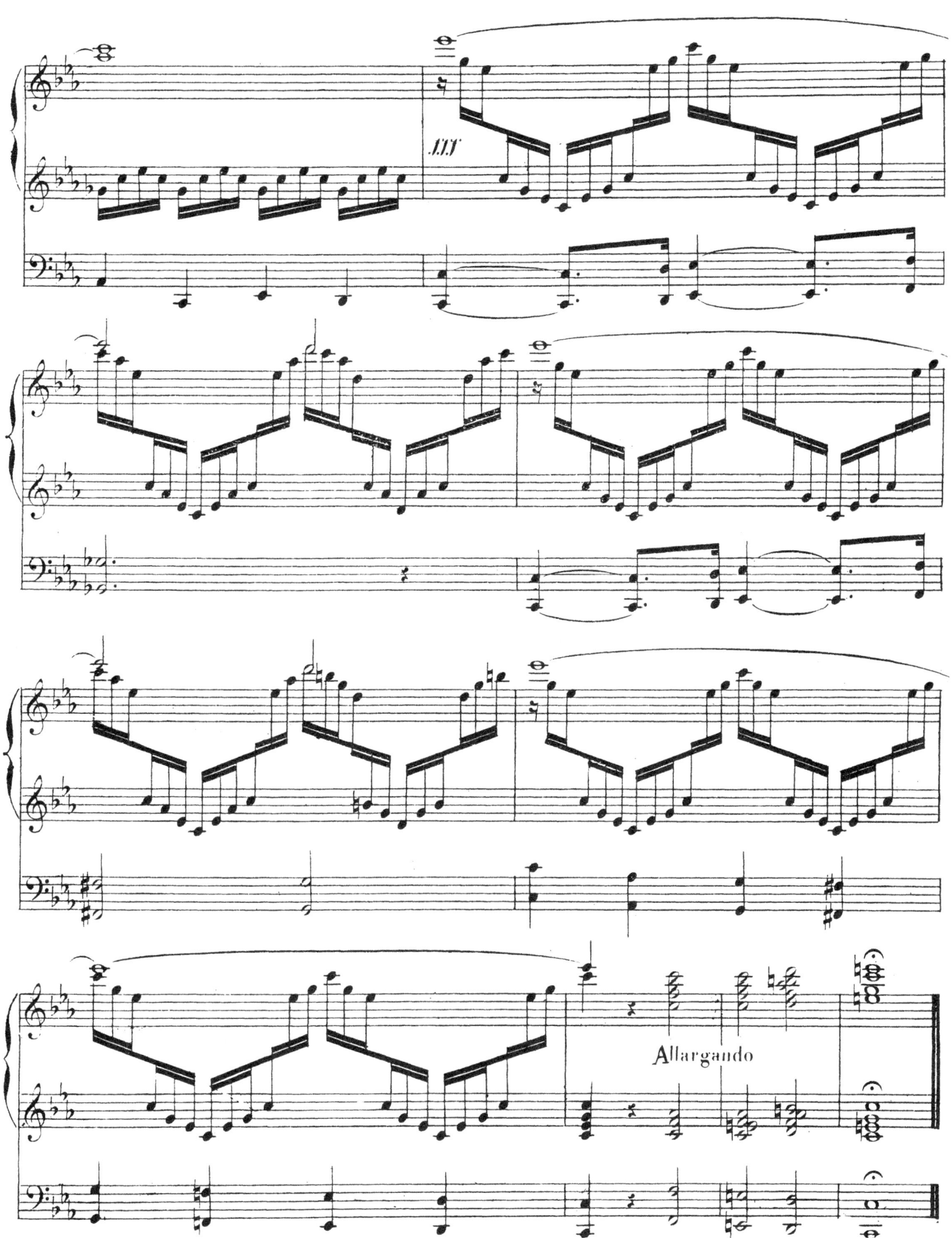

Boëllmann / 25

TOCCATA

Indication des Jeux. Fonds et anches à tous les claviers
Les Claviers accouplés.
Pédale, acc. au G. Orgue.

Joseph Callaerts
1838–1901

26

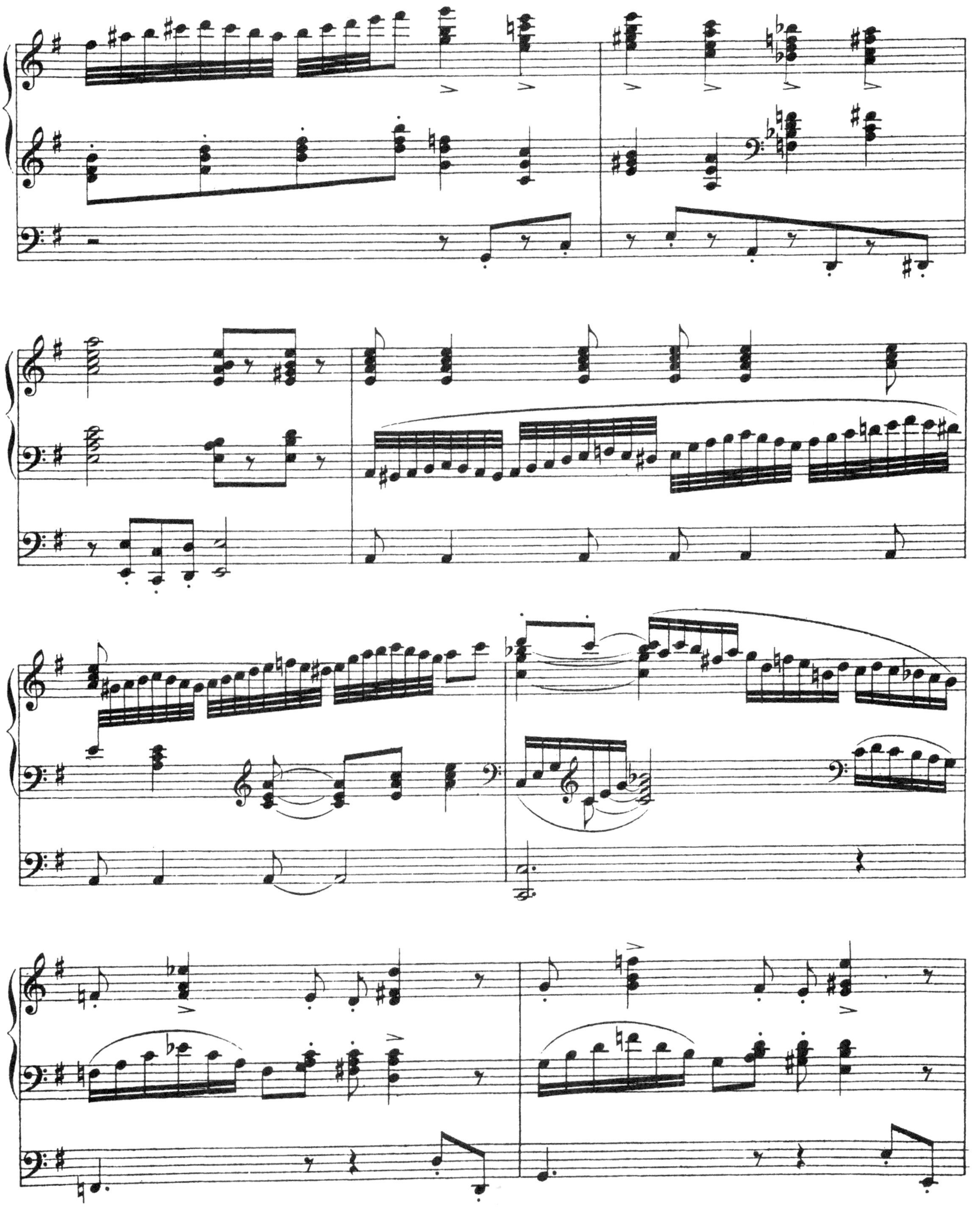

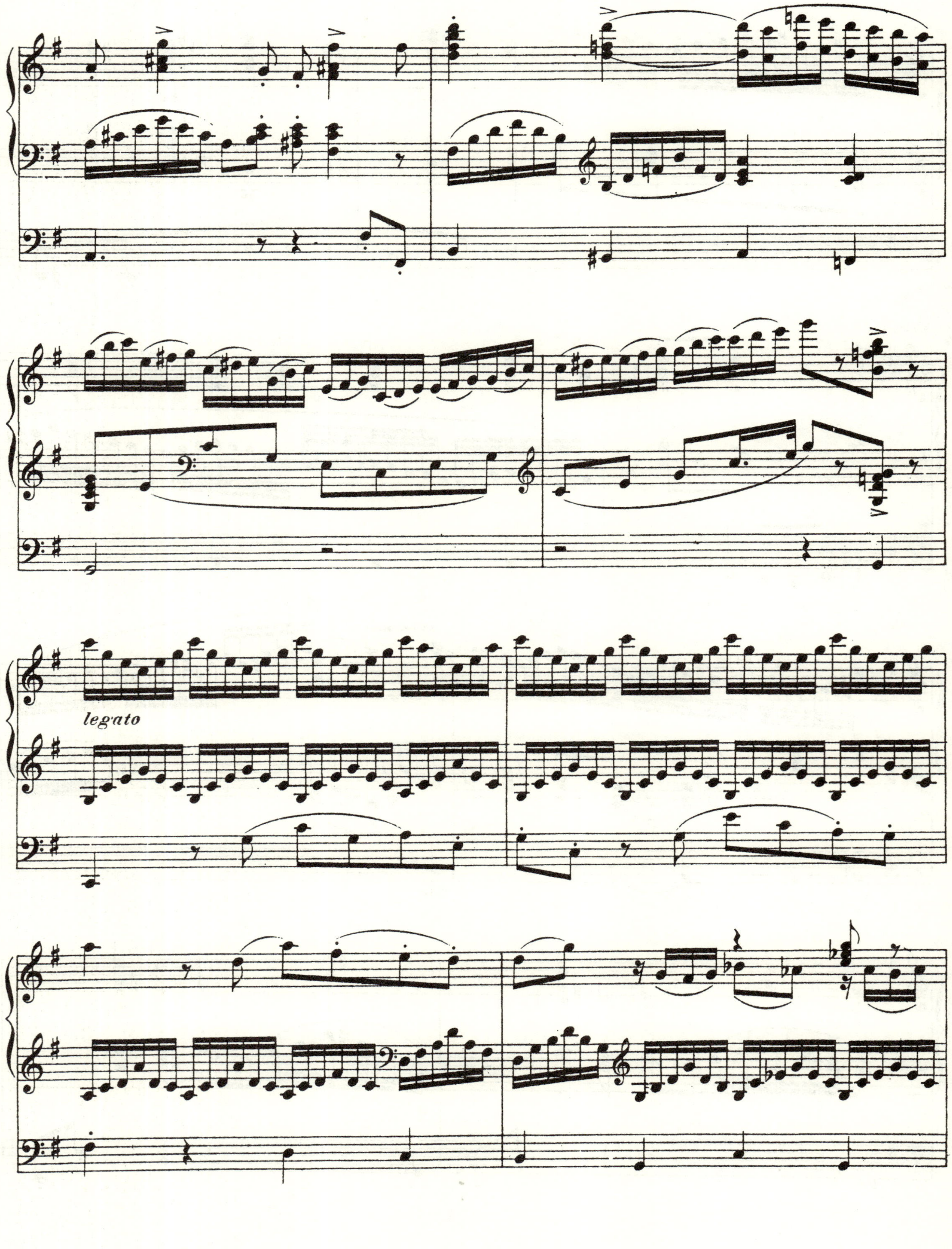
legato

Callaerts / 31

32 / Callaerts

TOCCATA

Théodore Dubois
1837–1924

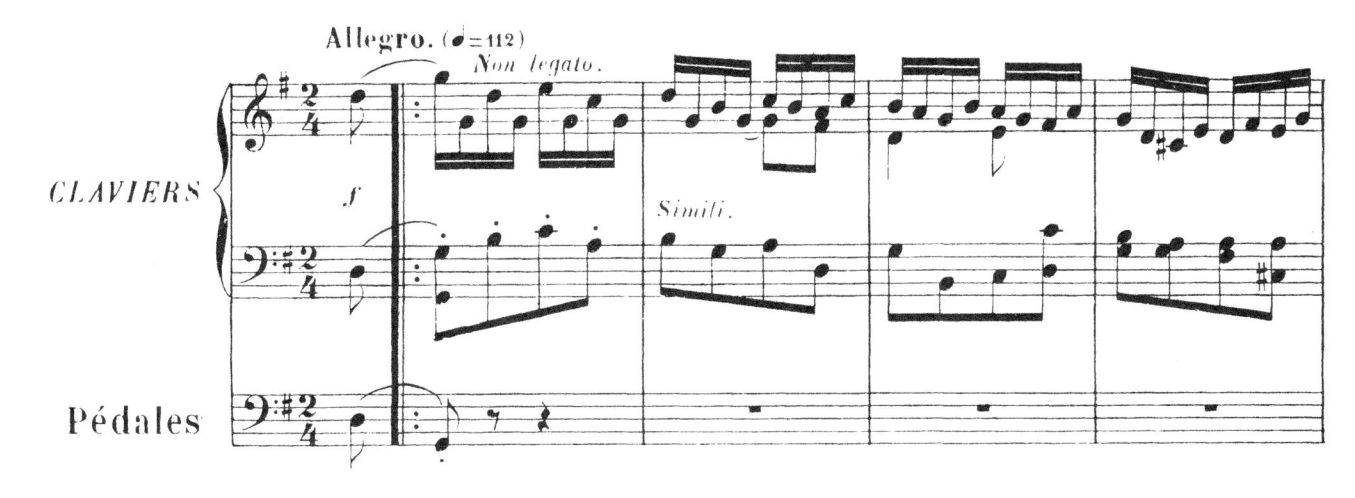

34 / Dubois

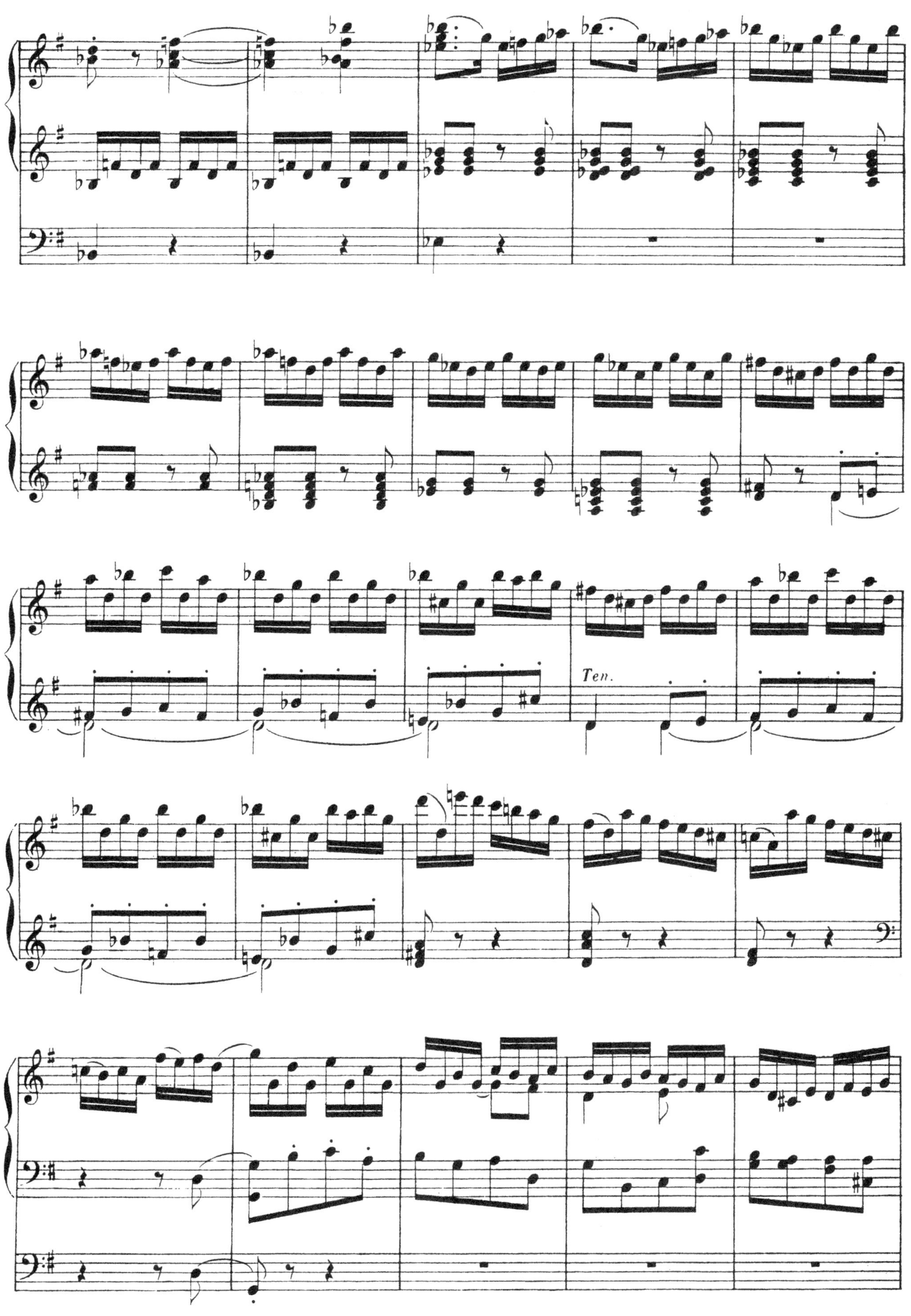
Ten.

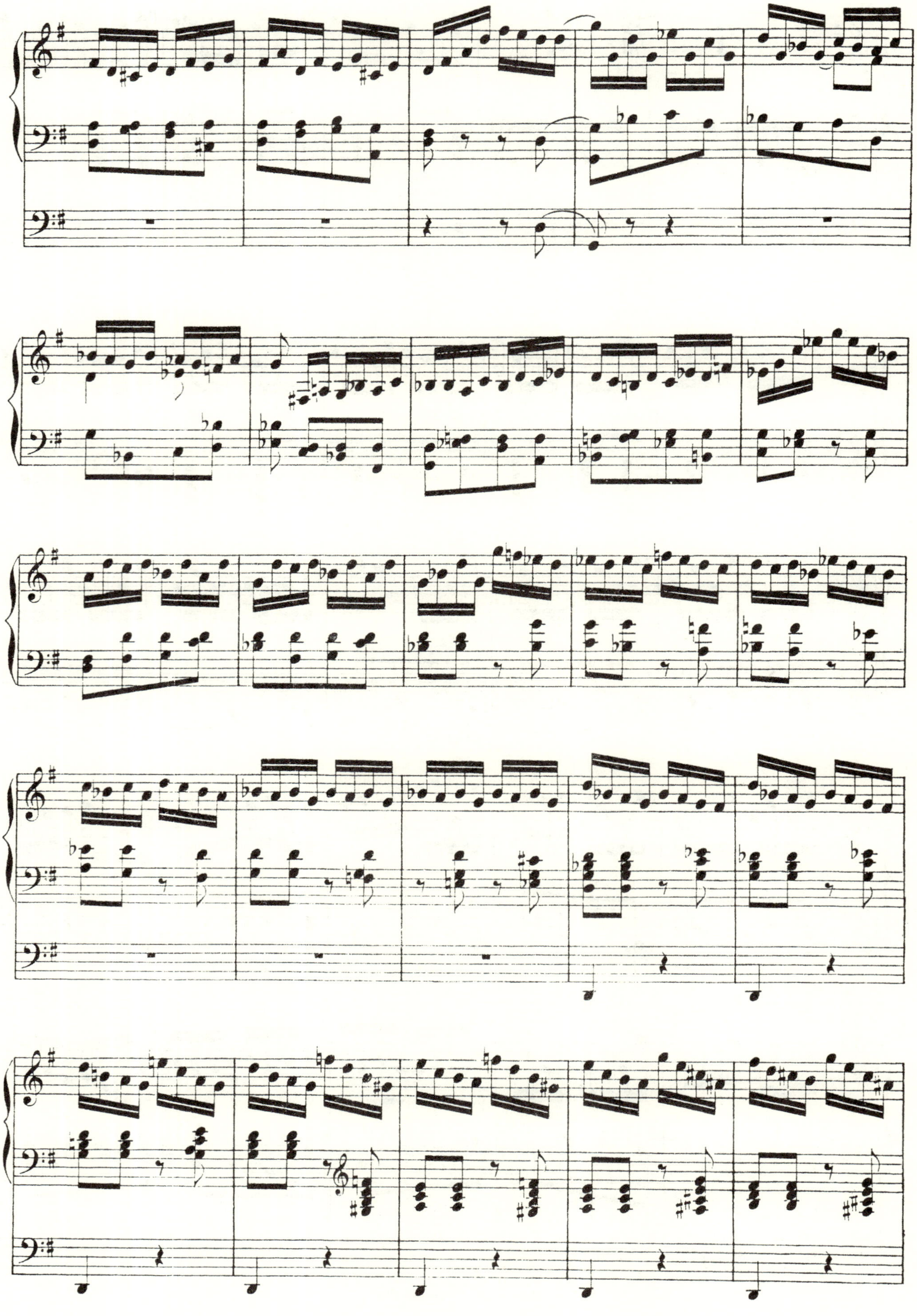

Dubois / 37

38 / Dubois

Dubois / 39

40 / Dubois

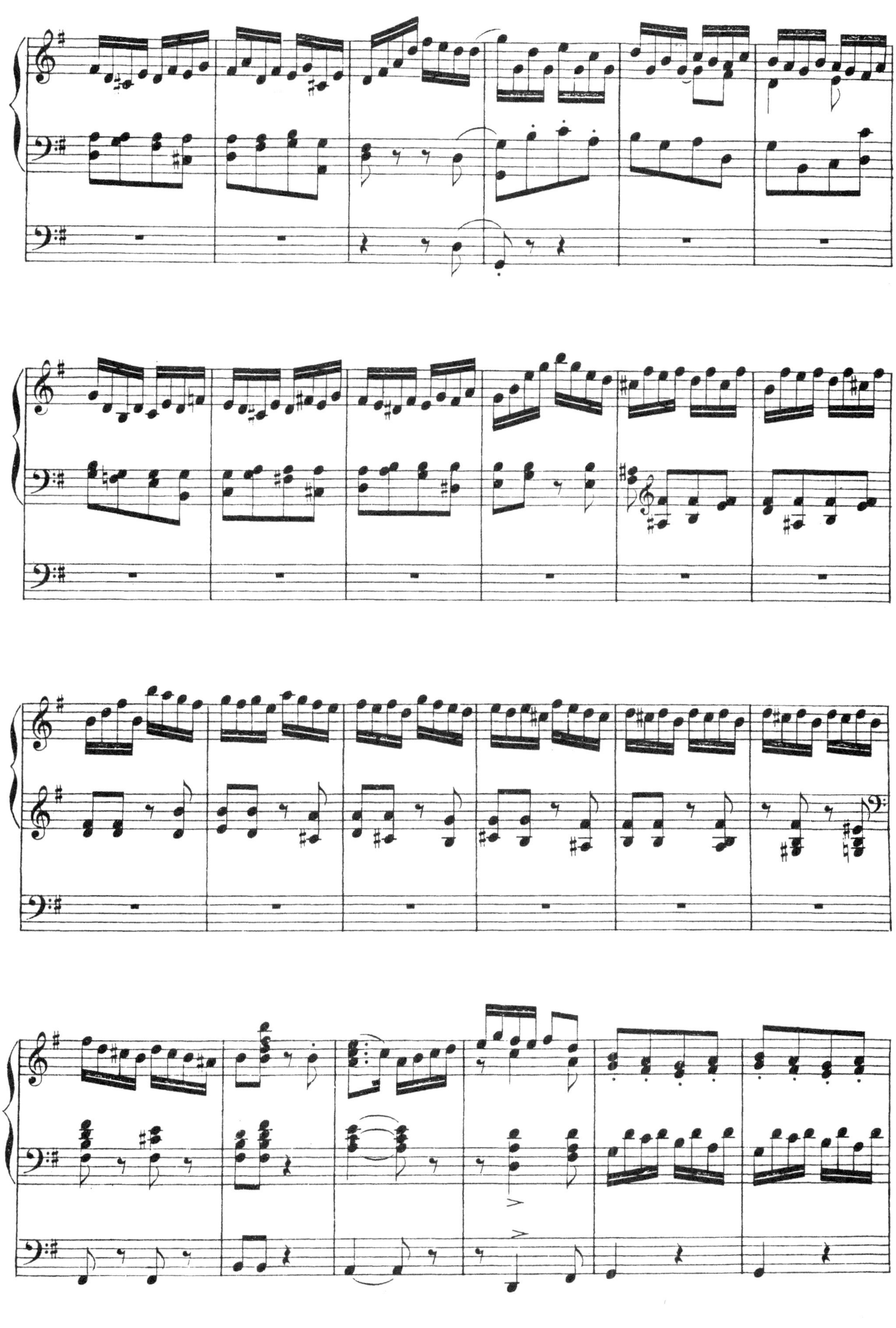

42 / Dubois

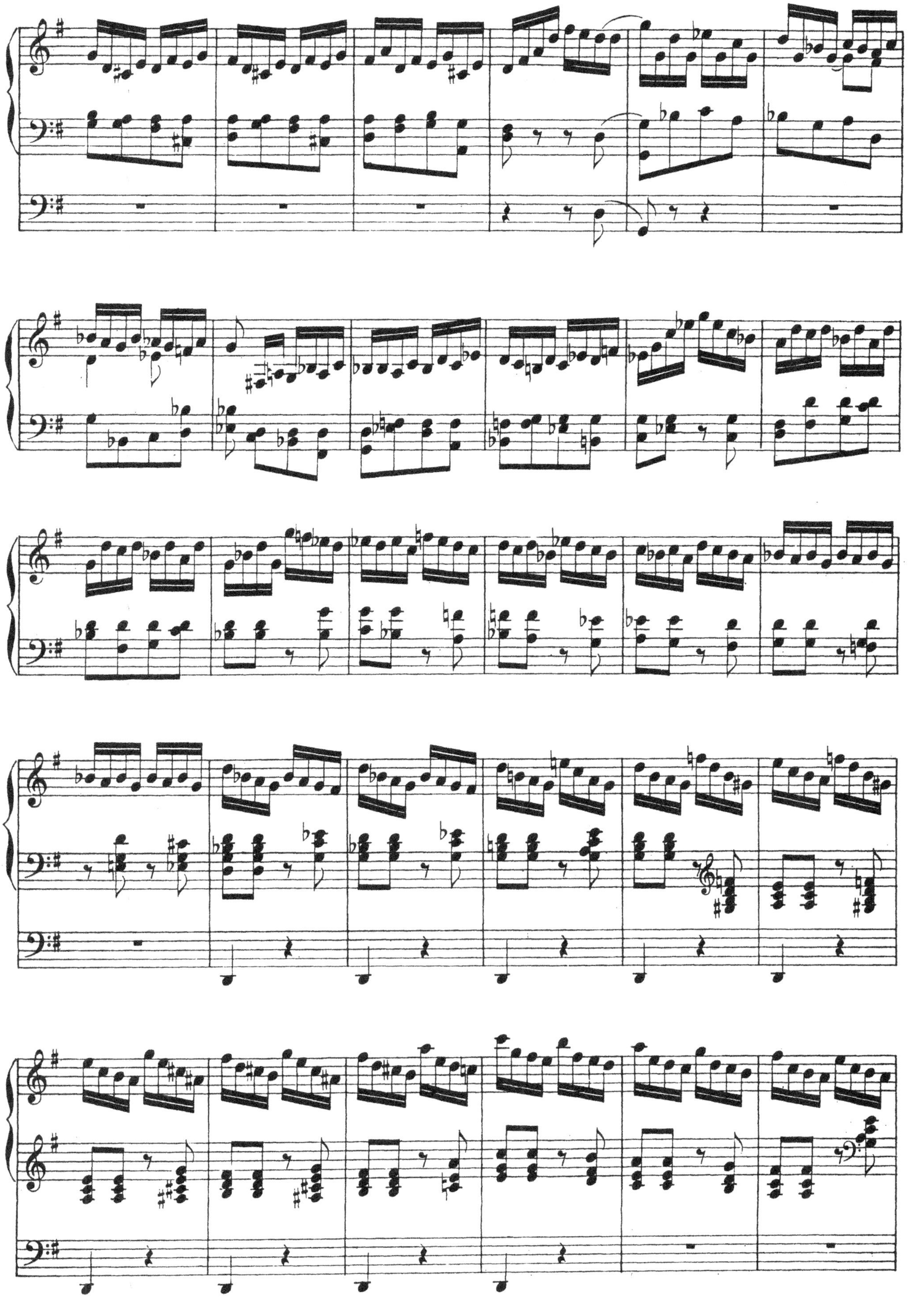

Ajoutez les 16 p. et peu à peu toute la force.

44 / *Dubois*

FESTIVAL TOCCATA

Prepare.
Swell.   Full. Box open.
Great. f 8 & 4 f^t, Sw. coupled.
Choir. mf 8, 4 & 2 f^t
Pedal. f 16 & 8 f^t, Gt. & Sw. coupled.

Percy E. Fletcher
1879–1932

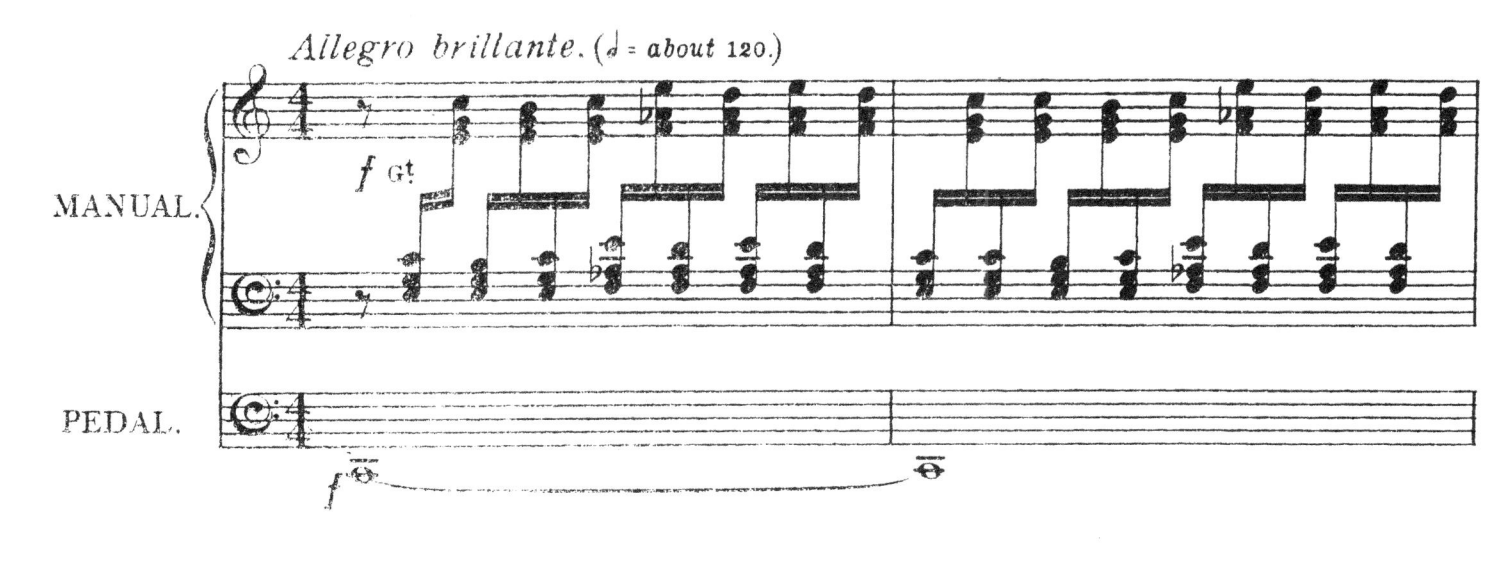

46 / Fletcher

Fletcher / 47

48 / Fletcher

Fletcher / 49

50 / Fletcher

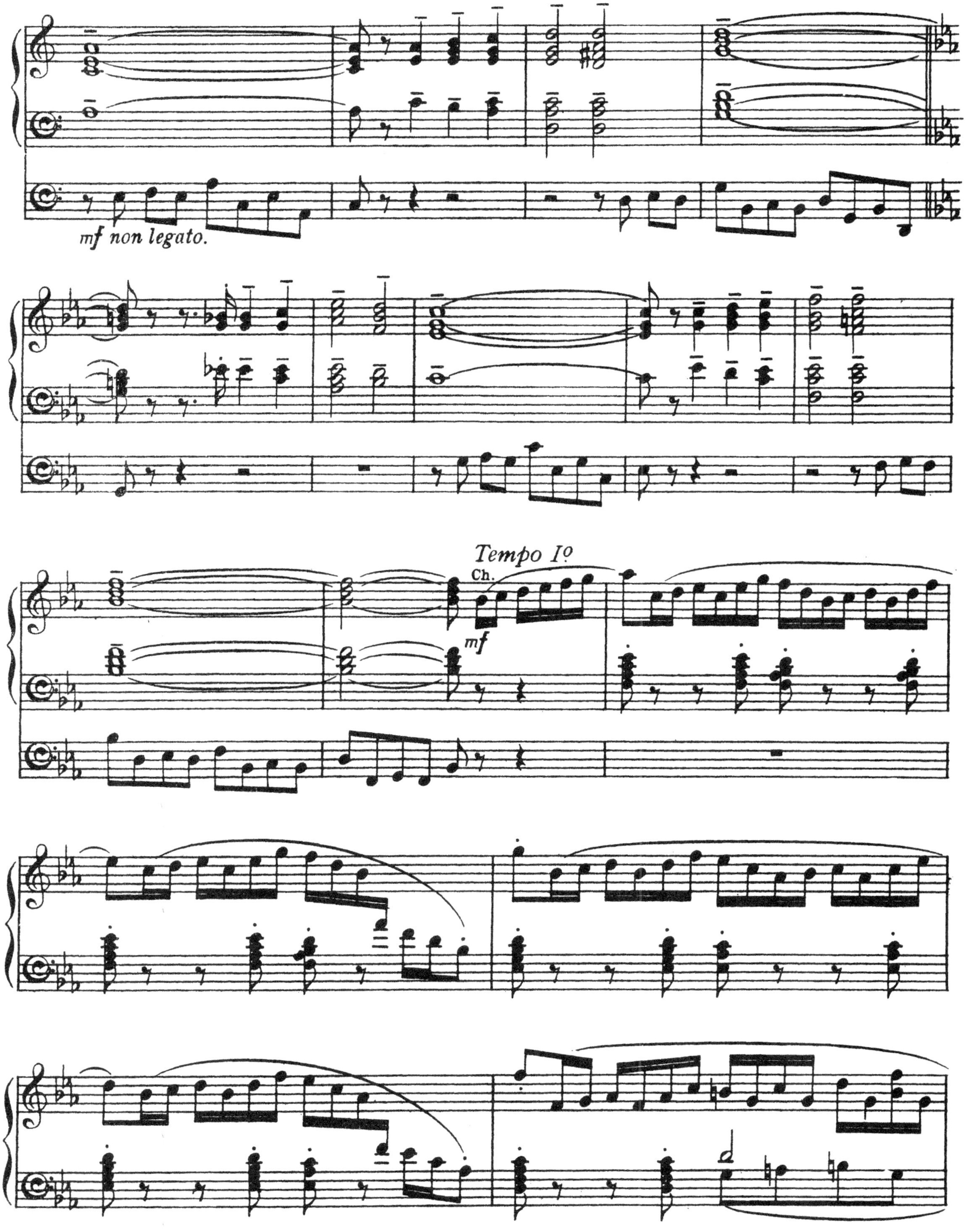
mf non legato.
Tempo I°
Ch.
mf

52 / Fletcher

a tempo un poco maestoso.

rit.

f Gt. 8ft. Reed. (or Solo Tuba.)

Ped.

f

54 / Fletcher

Fletcher / 55

56 / *Fletcher*

Fletcher / 57

58 / Fletcher

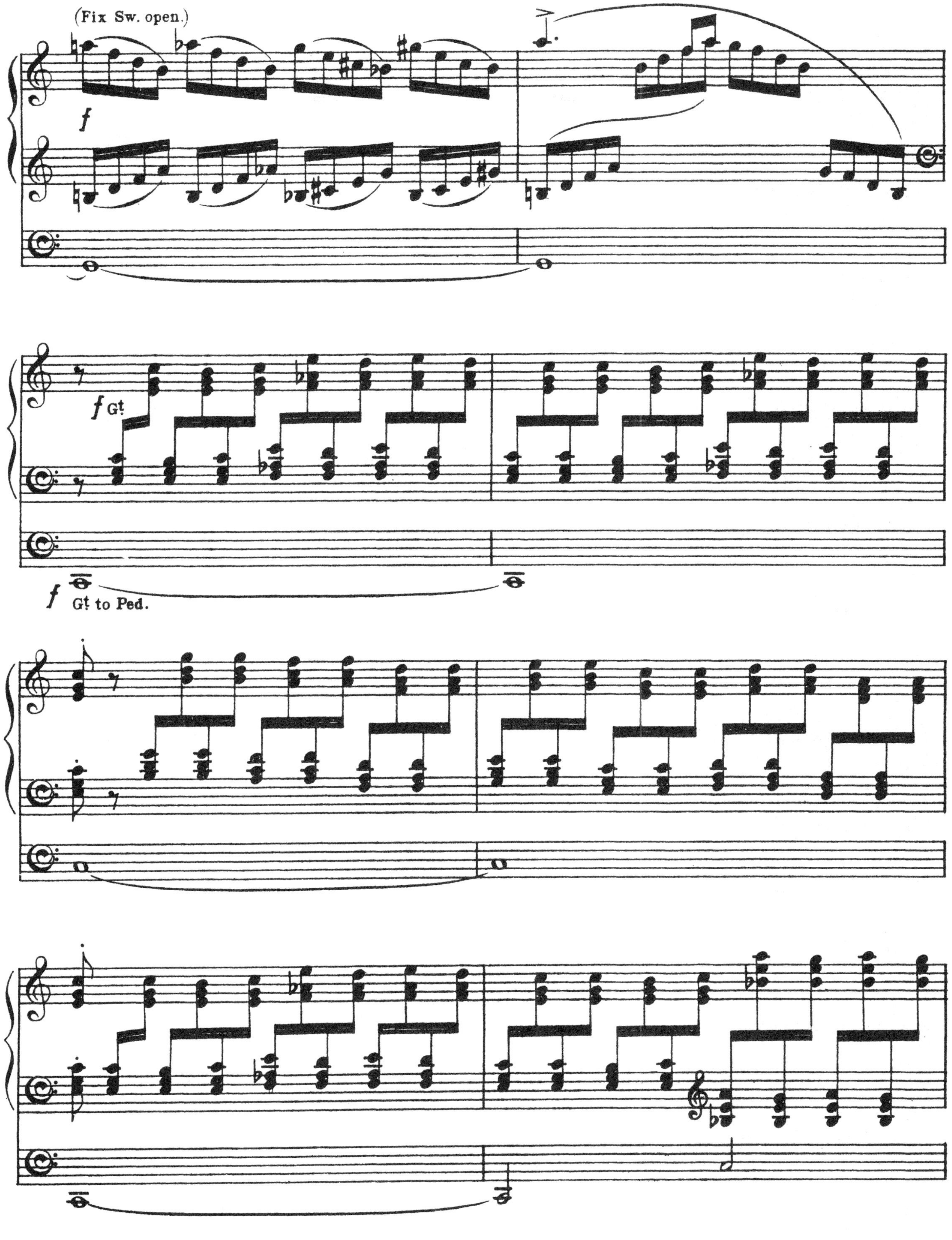
(Fix Sw. open.)
f
f Gt
f Gt to Ped.

60 / Fletcher

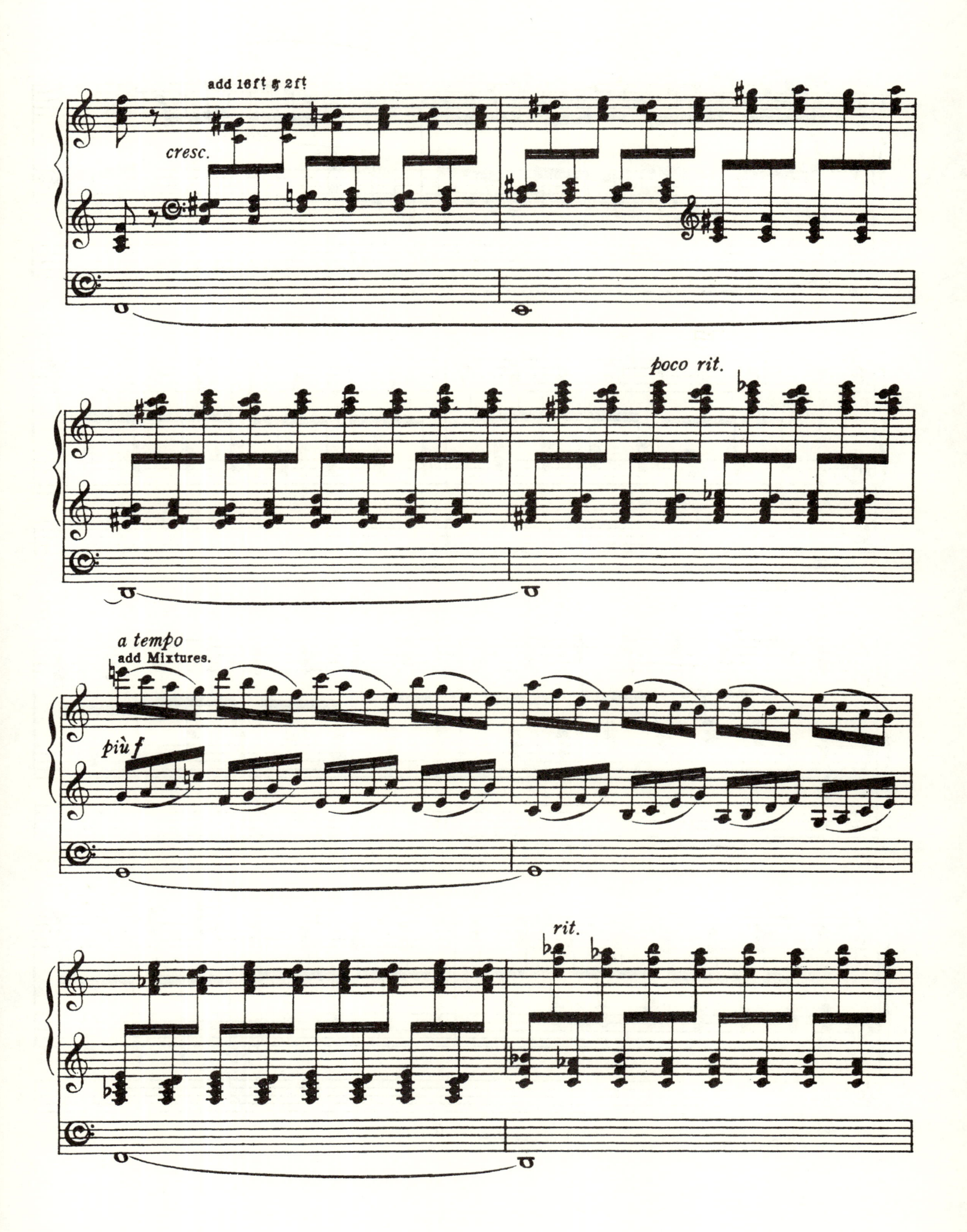

Fletcher / 61

à Clarence Eddy

TOCCATA

Au Grand Orgue et au Positif les Fonds de 8 et 4 P. (puis les
Anches de 8 et 4 P.) _ Au Récit, les Fonds et les Anches de 8 et 4 P.
A la Pédale, les Fonds de 16, 8, 4 P. (puis les Anches de 16, 8, 4 P.).

Eugène Gigout
1844–1925

Allegro.
Récit et Pos.*)

MANUALE

Les Fonds de 8 et 4 p. avec les Anches 8 et 4 p. du Récit (boîte fermée)

Pédale

(*) Jouer le Récit et le Positif accouplés au G.d Orgue, en neutralisant les Fonds de ce clavier.

Si l'on ne dispose que d'un orgue à deux claviers, il faudra commencer cette pièce par le G.d Orgue (avec les Fonds seulement) et le Récit (Fonds et Anches) accouplés.

p Les Fonds.

64 / Gigout

Cre - *scen* -

Ajoutez les Anches du Positif.

- - - - - - - - - *do.*

Ajoutez les Fonds du G^d Orgue.

f Ajoutez les Anches.

66 / Gigout

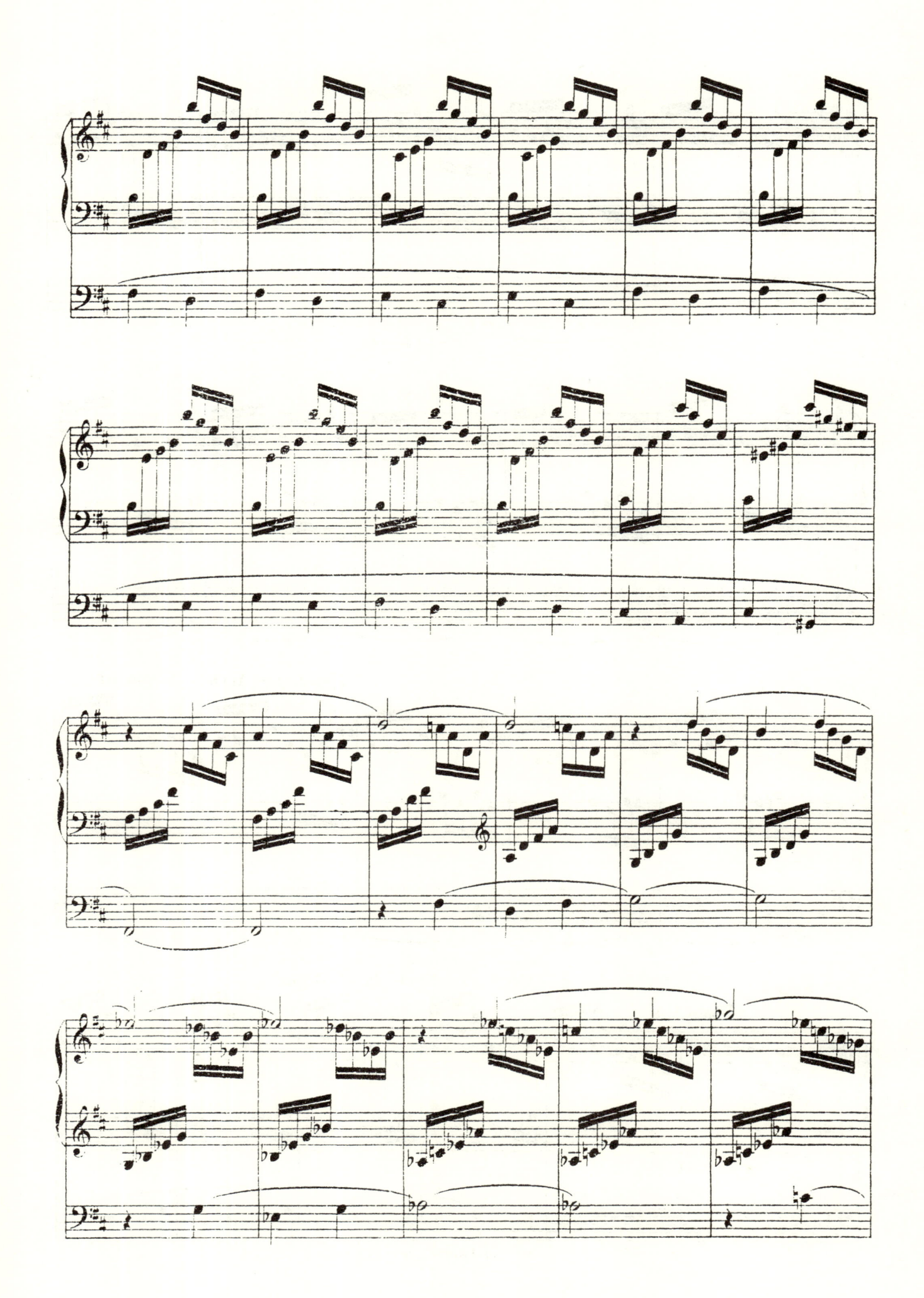

Gigout / 67

Ajoutez les Anches du G.d Orgue.

Tirasse.

68 / Gigout

Gigout / 69

Allargando.

Ajoutez les 16 p.

70 / Gigout

à William C. Carl

TOCCATA
Op. 67, No. 2

RÉC.
POS. } Grand Chœur;
G. } Claviers accouplés.
PÉD.   16. 8. Tirasse G. Anches préparées.

SW.
G. } Full Organ;
CH. } Manuals coupled.
PED.   16. 8. G⁺ to Ped. Without Reeds.

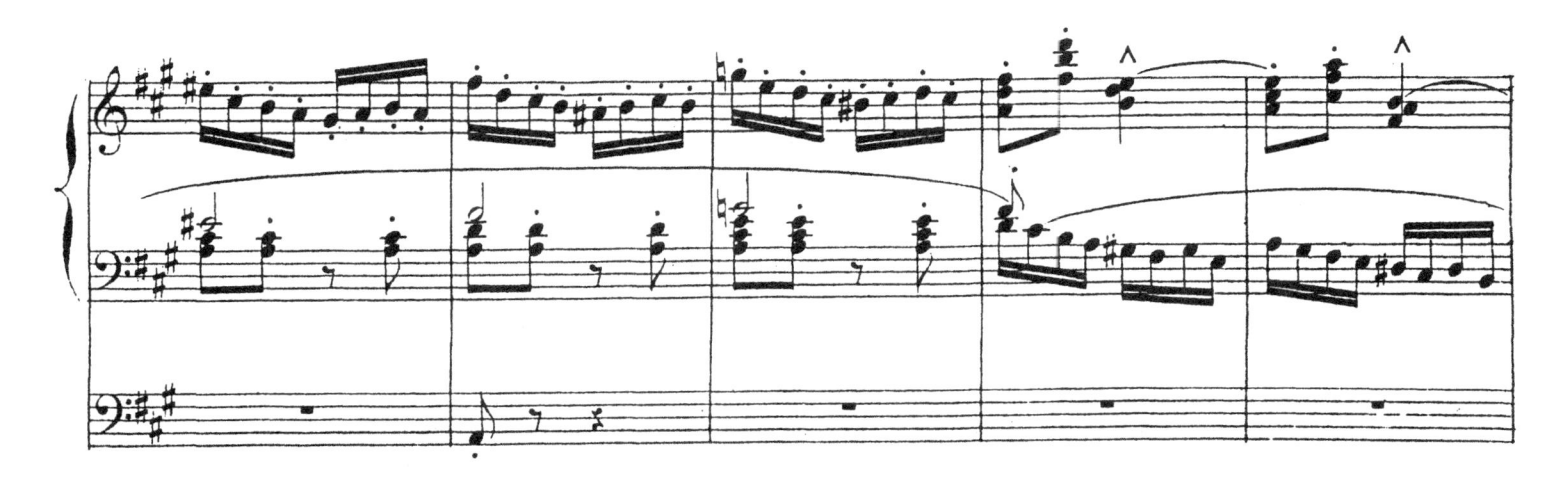

Georges MacMaster
1862–1898

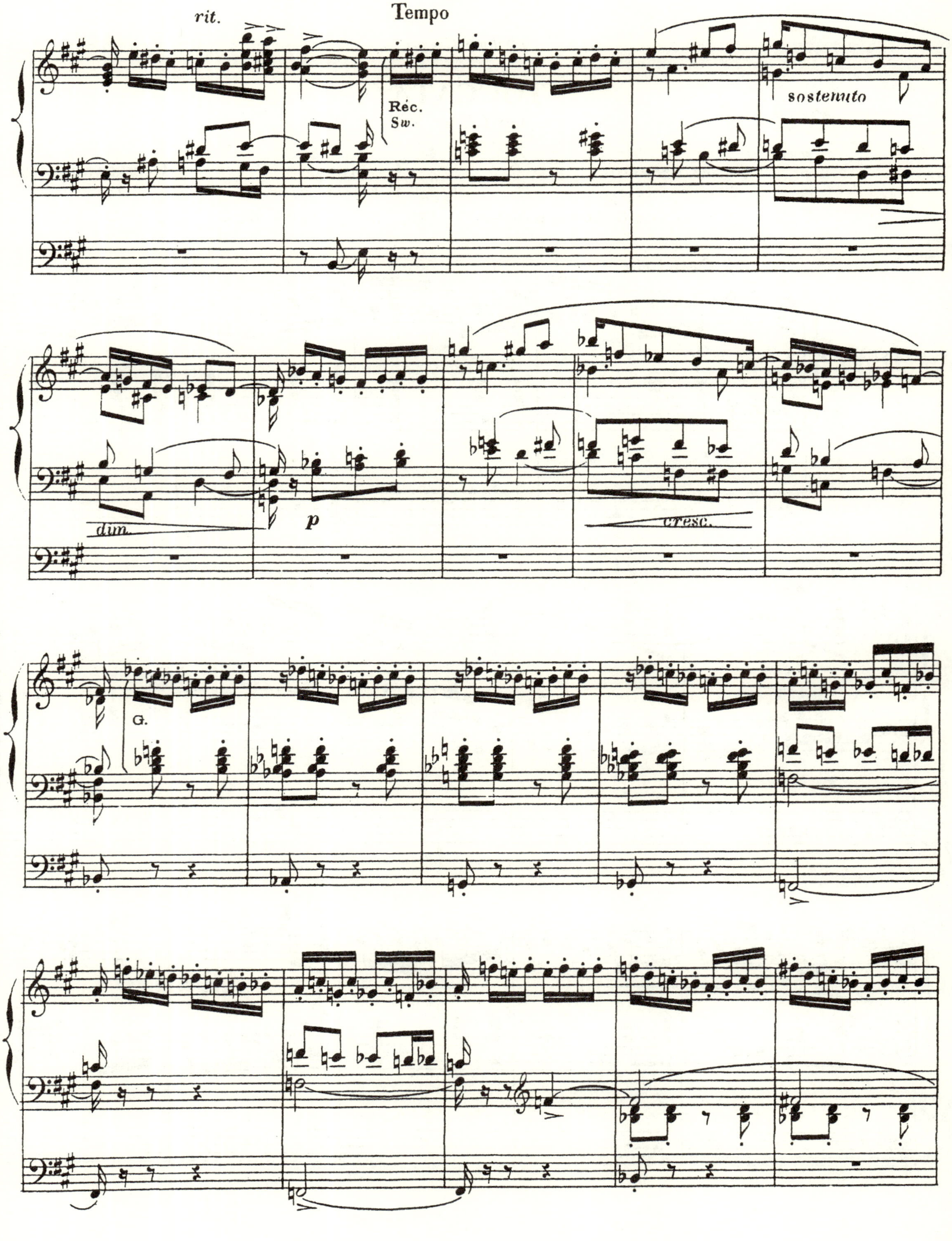

rit.
Tempo
Réc.
Sw.
sostenuto
dim.
p
cresc.
G.

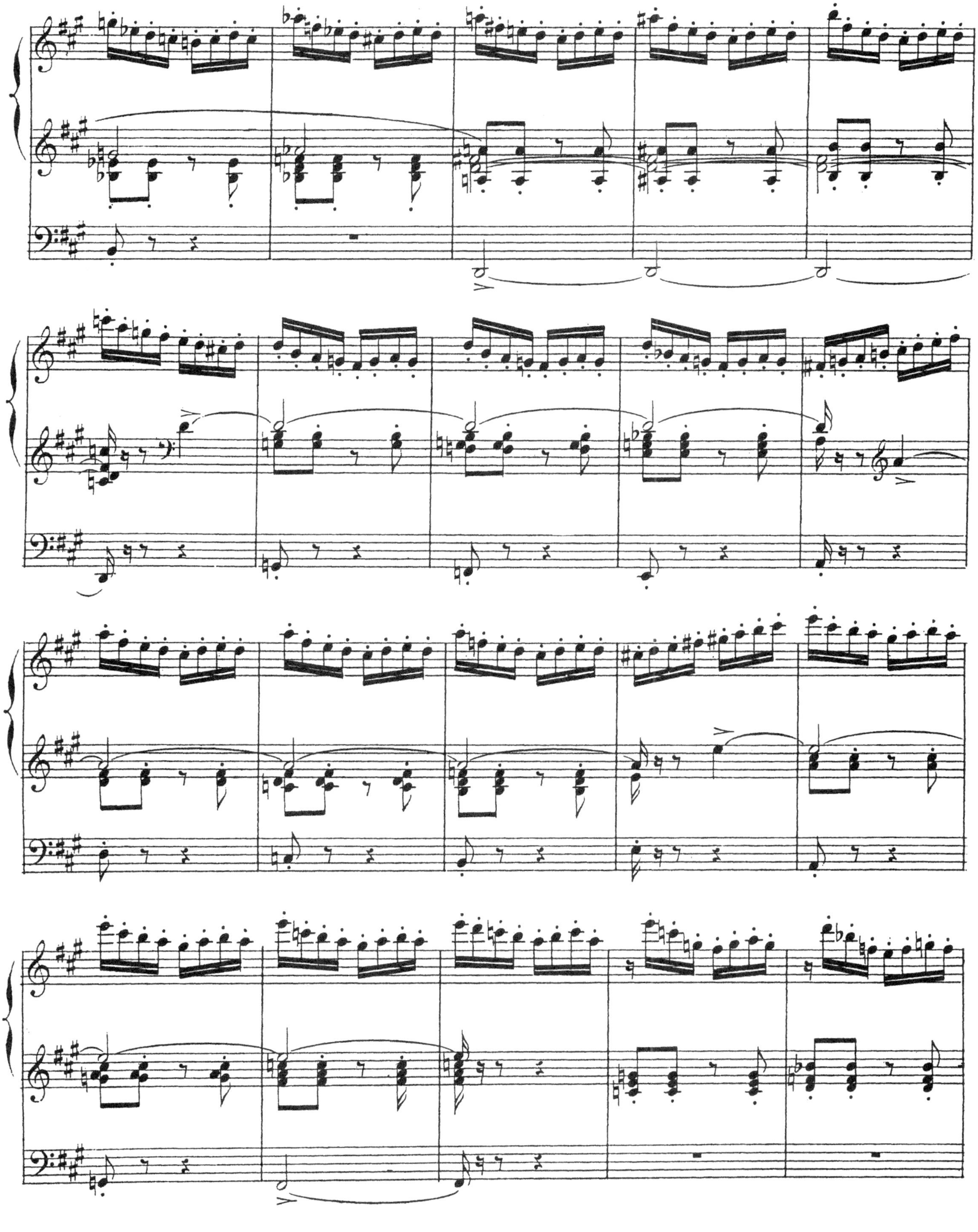

74 / MacMaster

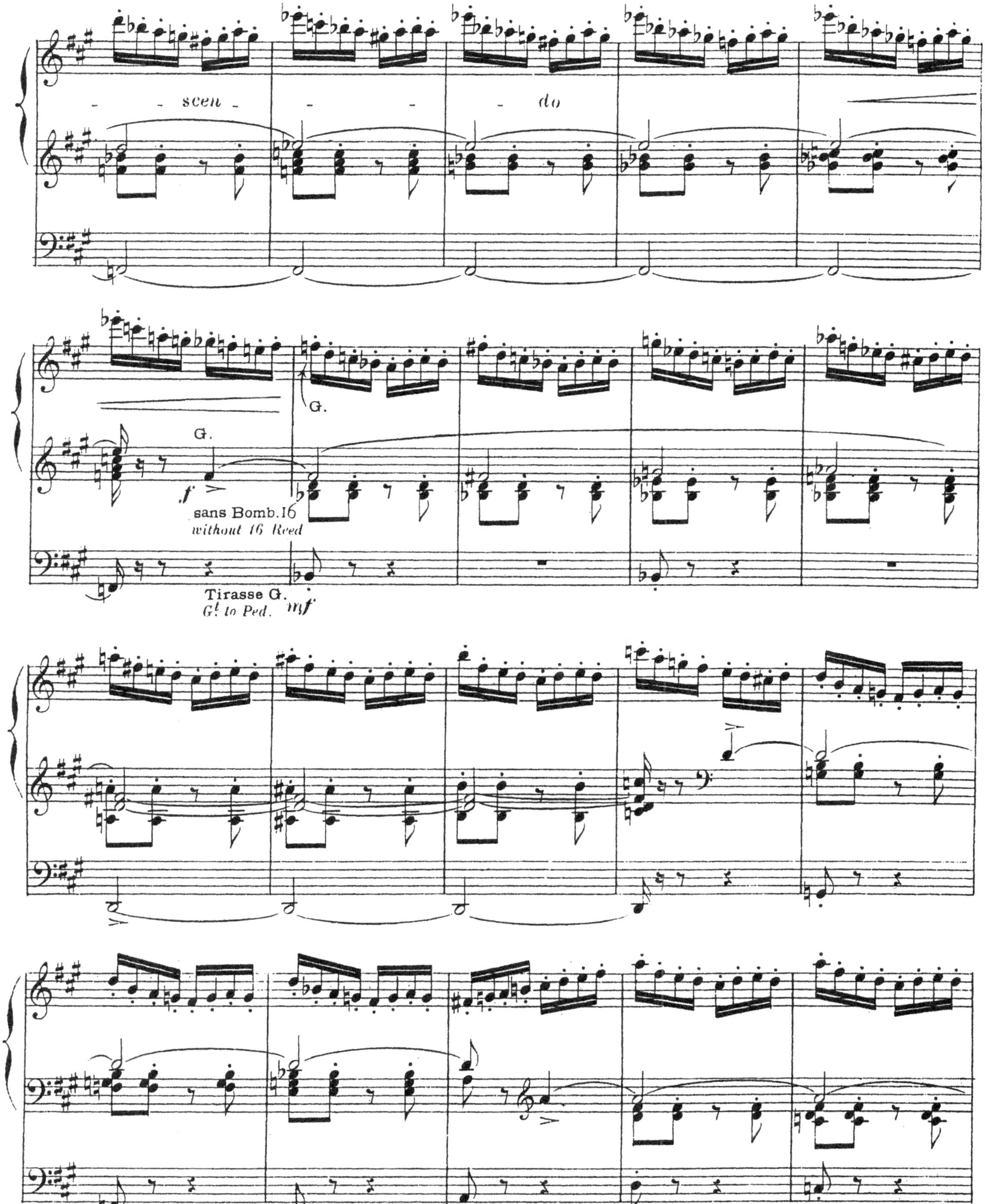
- - scen - - - do
G.
G.
f
sans Bomb.16
without 16 Reed
Tirasse G.
Gt to Ped.
mf

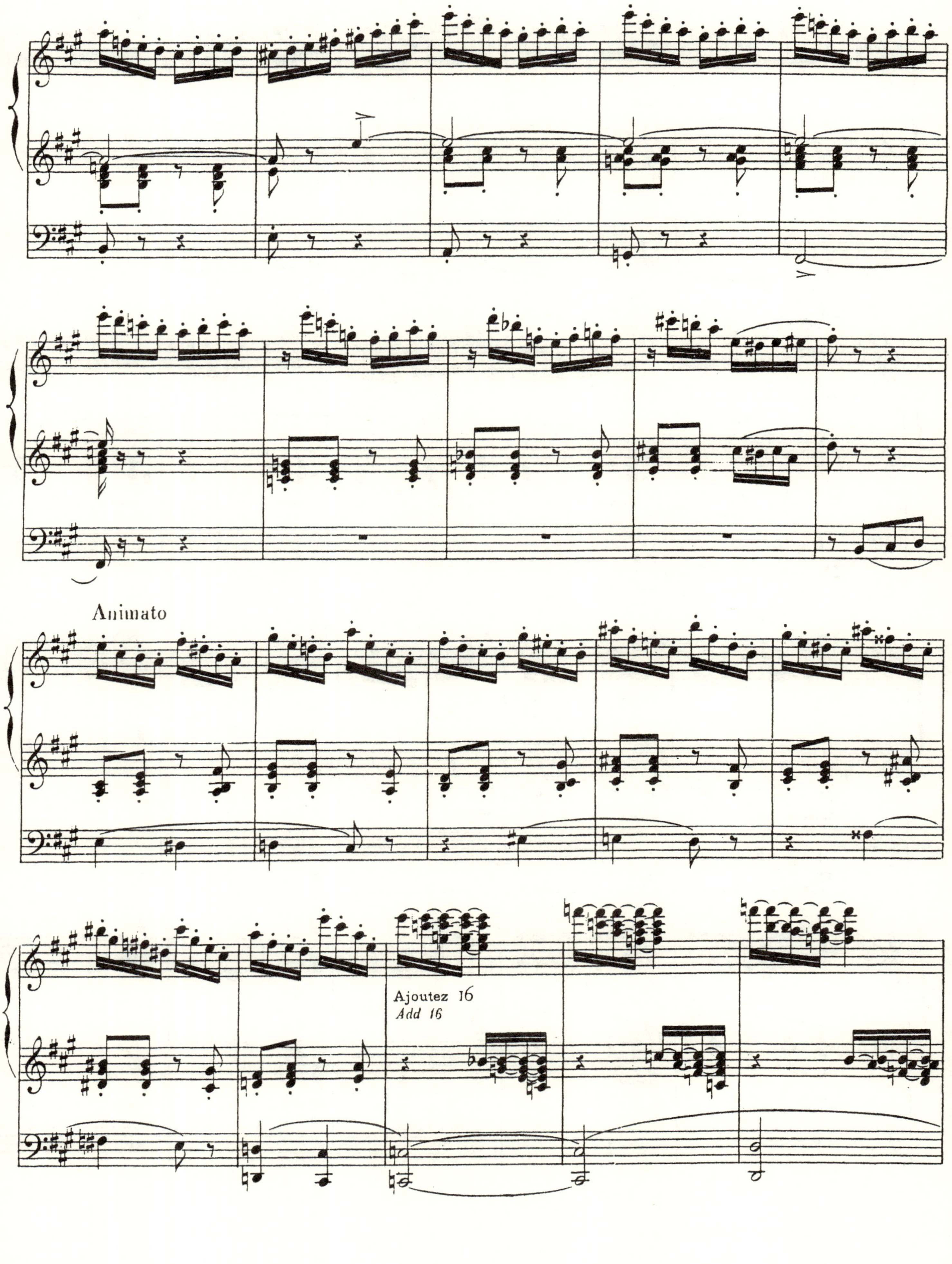
Animato
Ajoutez 16
Add 16

Largo
tutti forza
ff
Anches
Reeds
POS. ou RÉC.
CH. or SW.
tr
G.
Allargando

à W.T. Best

TOCCATA

Grand Chœur. Tous les Claviers accouplés. (Sans 16')

Alphonse Mailly
1833–1918

Allegro con fuoco

sempre staccato

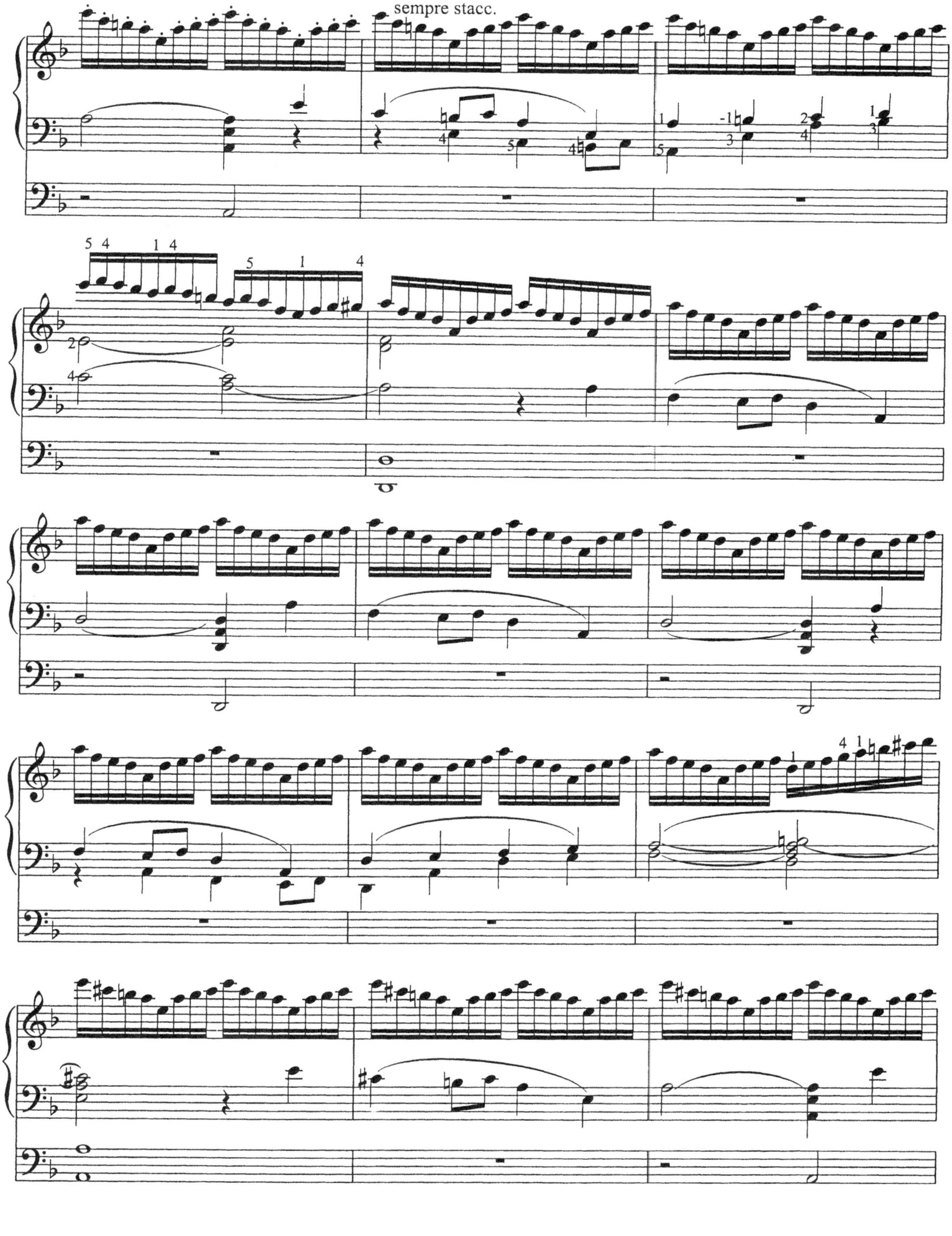
sempre stacc.

80 / Mailly

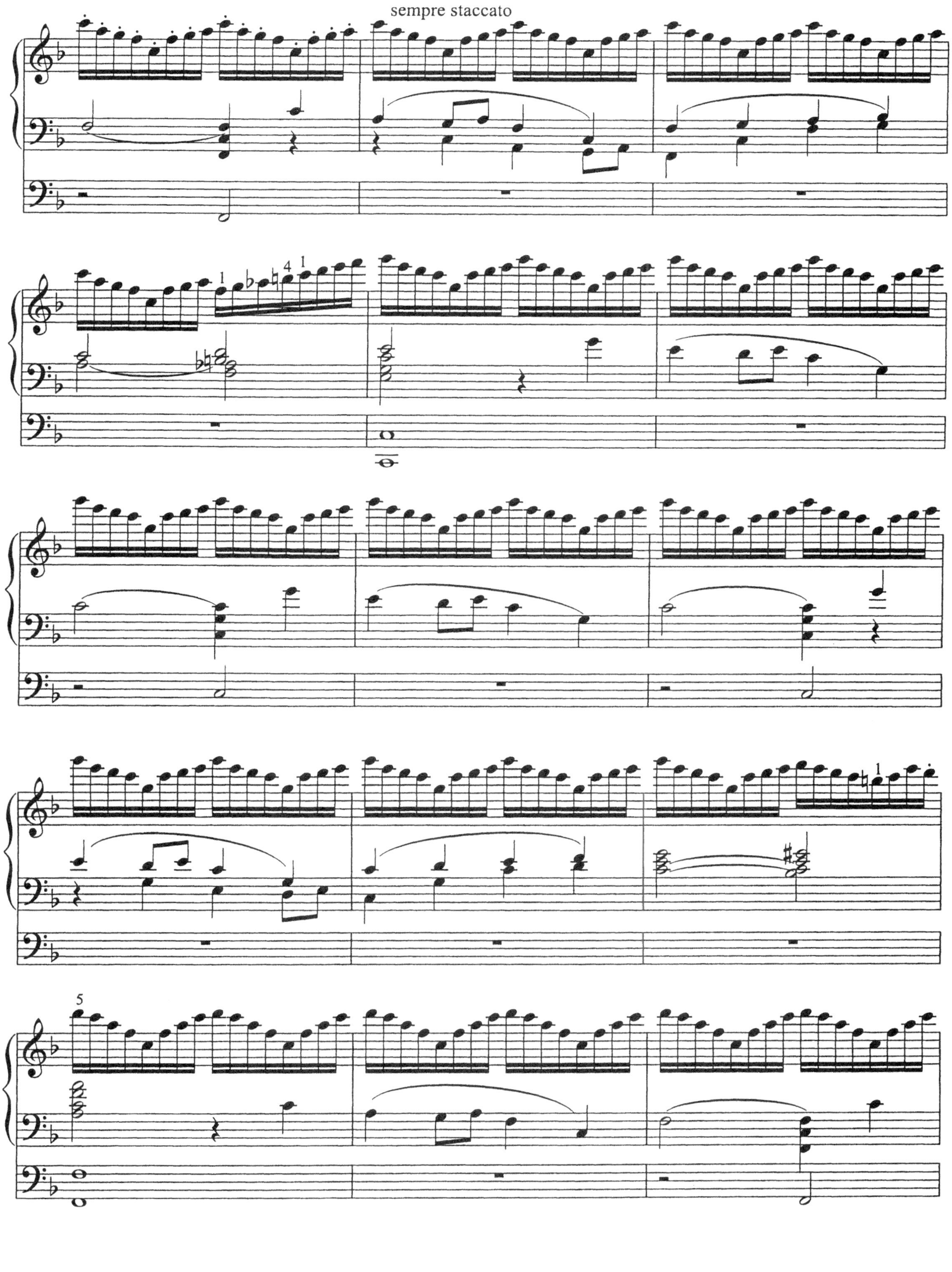
sempre staccato

82 / Mailly

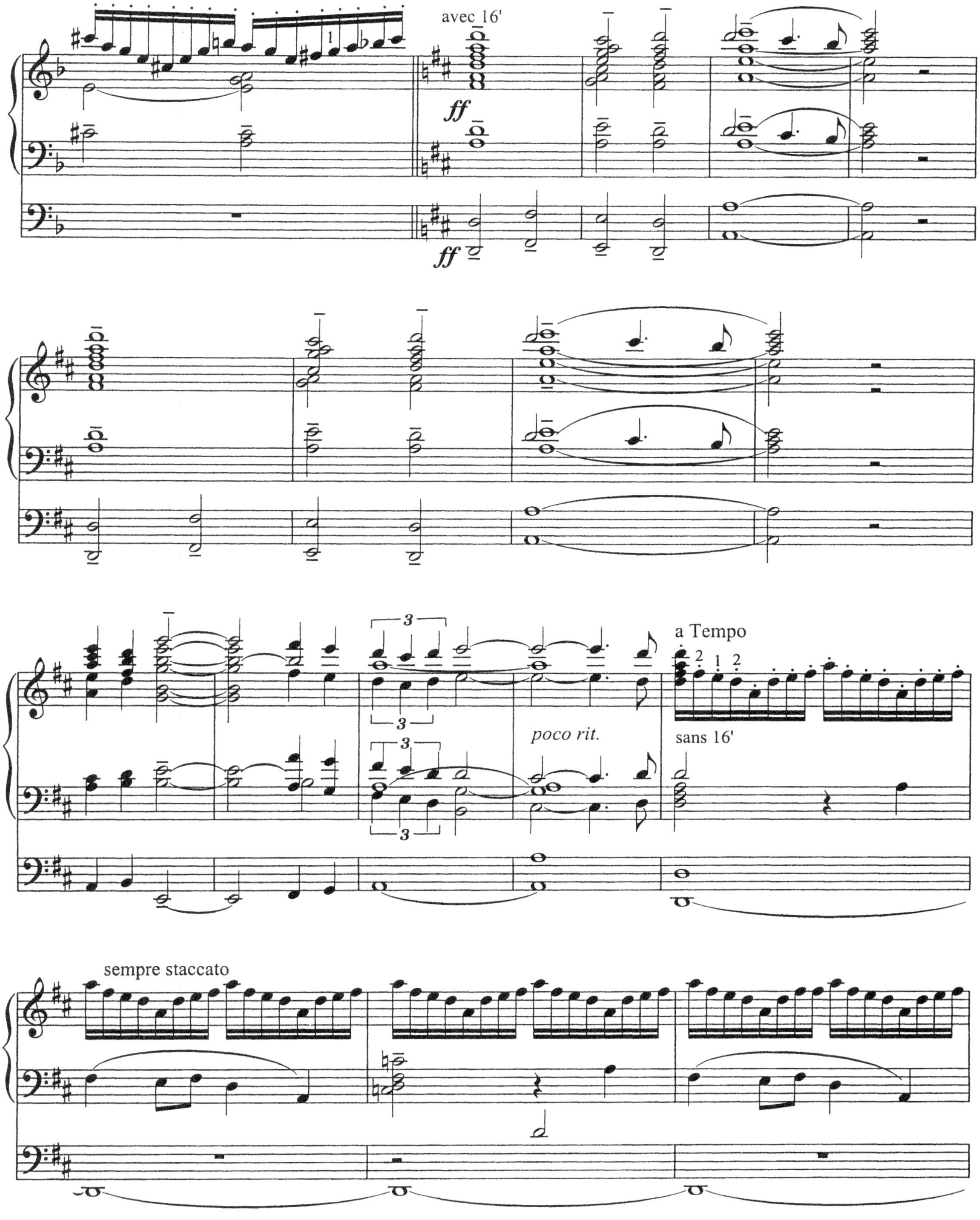
avec 16'
ff
ff
a Tempo
poco rit.
sans 16'
sempre staccato

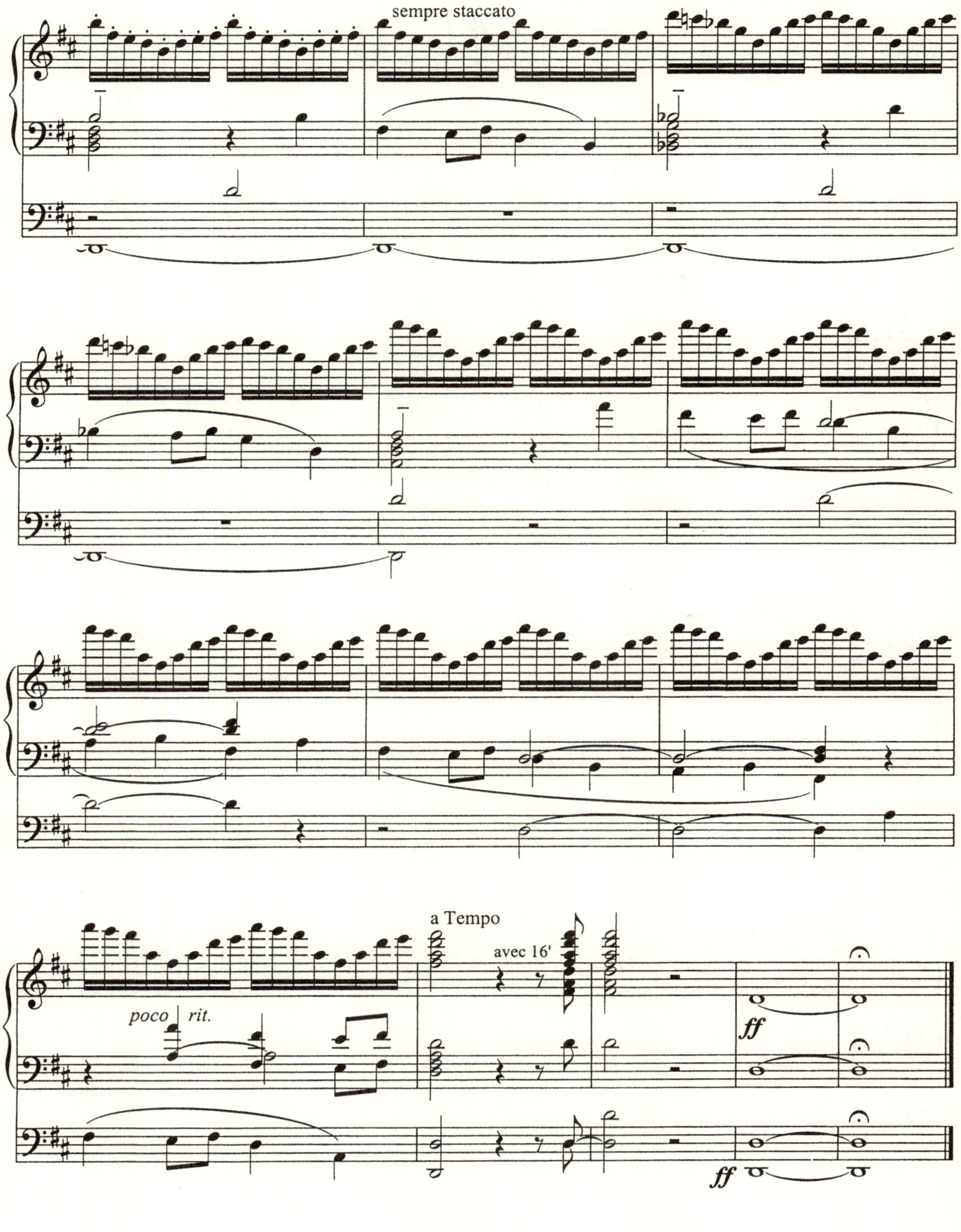
sempre staccato
poco rit.
a Tempo
avec 16'
ff
ff

Tu es petra et portæ
inferi non prævalebunt adversus te

G. et P. Fonds 8, 4, 16
R.   Fonds et anches 8, 4, 16
          et mutations
Péd.   Fonds 8, 4, 16, 32

Henri Mulet
1887–1967

86 / Mulet

Mulet / 87

88 / Mulet

Mulet / 89

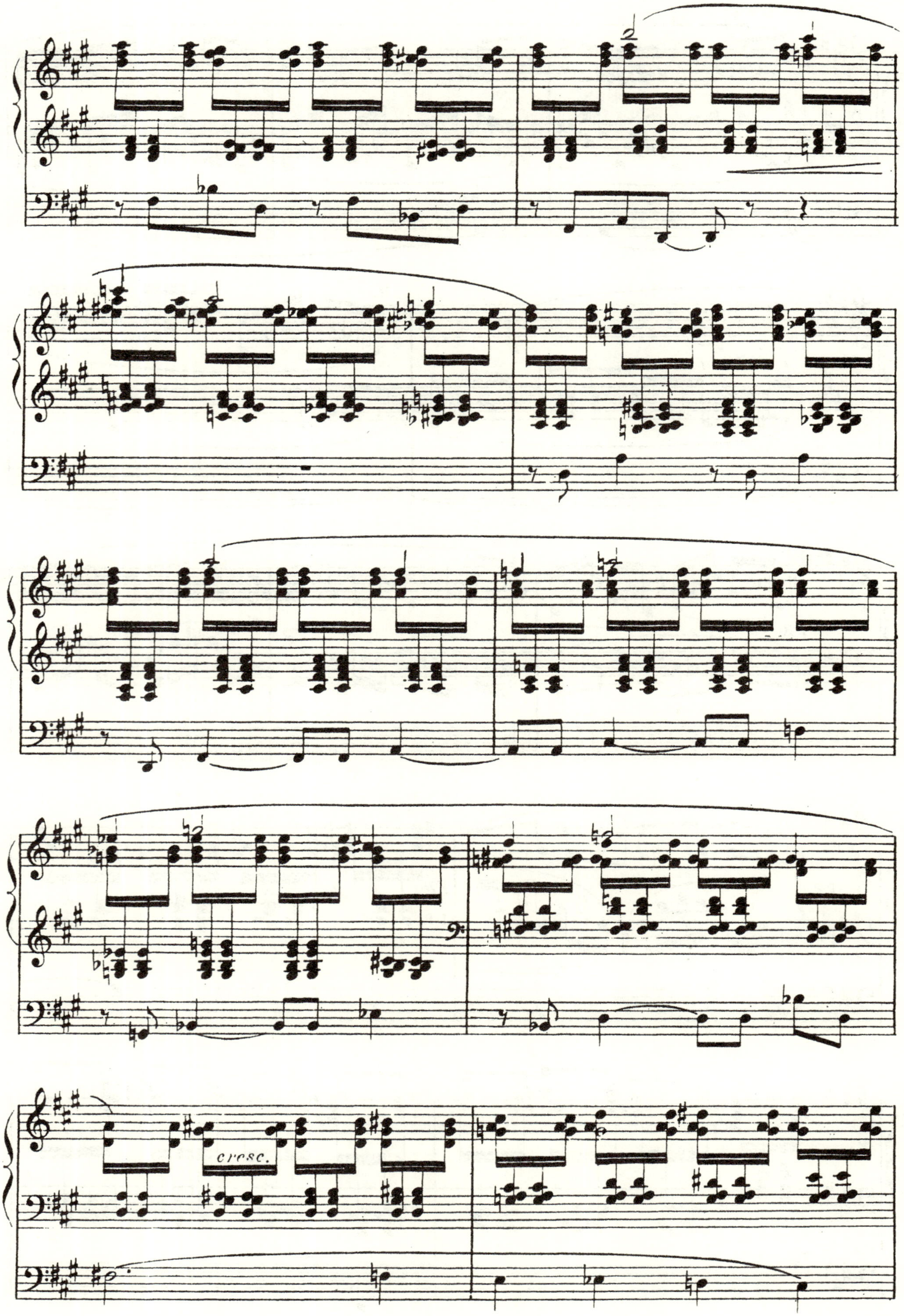
cresc.

Mulet / 91

92 / Mulet

Mulet / 93

Mettez la Bombarde au G.

94 / *Mulet*

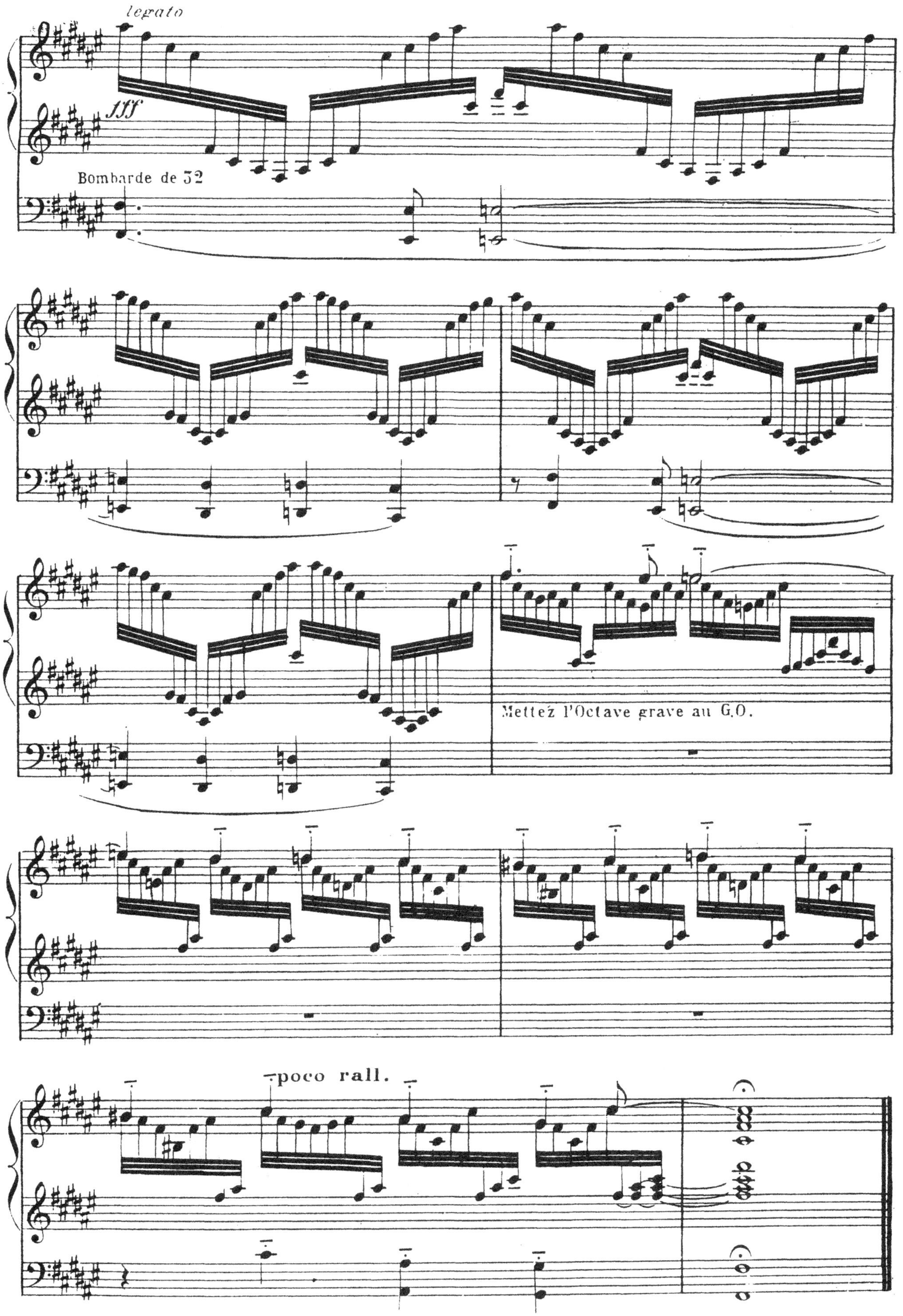
legato
fff
Bombarde de 32
Mettez l'Octave grave au G.O.
poco rall.

À ALEXANDRE GUILMANT
Professeur au Conservatoire National de Musique de Paris

TOCCATA EN RÉ MINEUR
Op. 108, No. 1

Albert Renaud
1855–1924

Renaud / 97

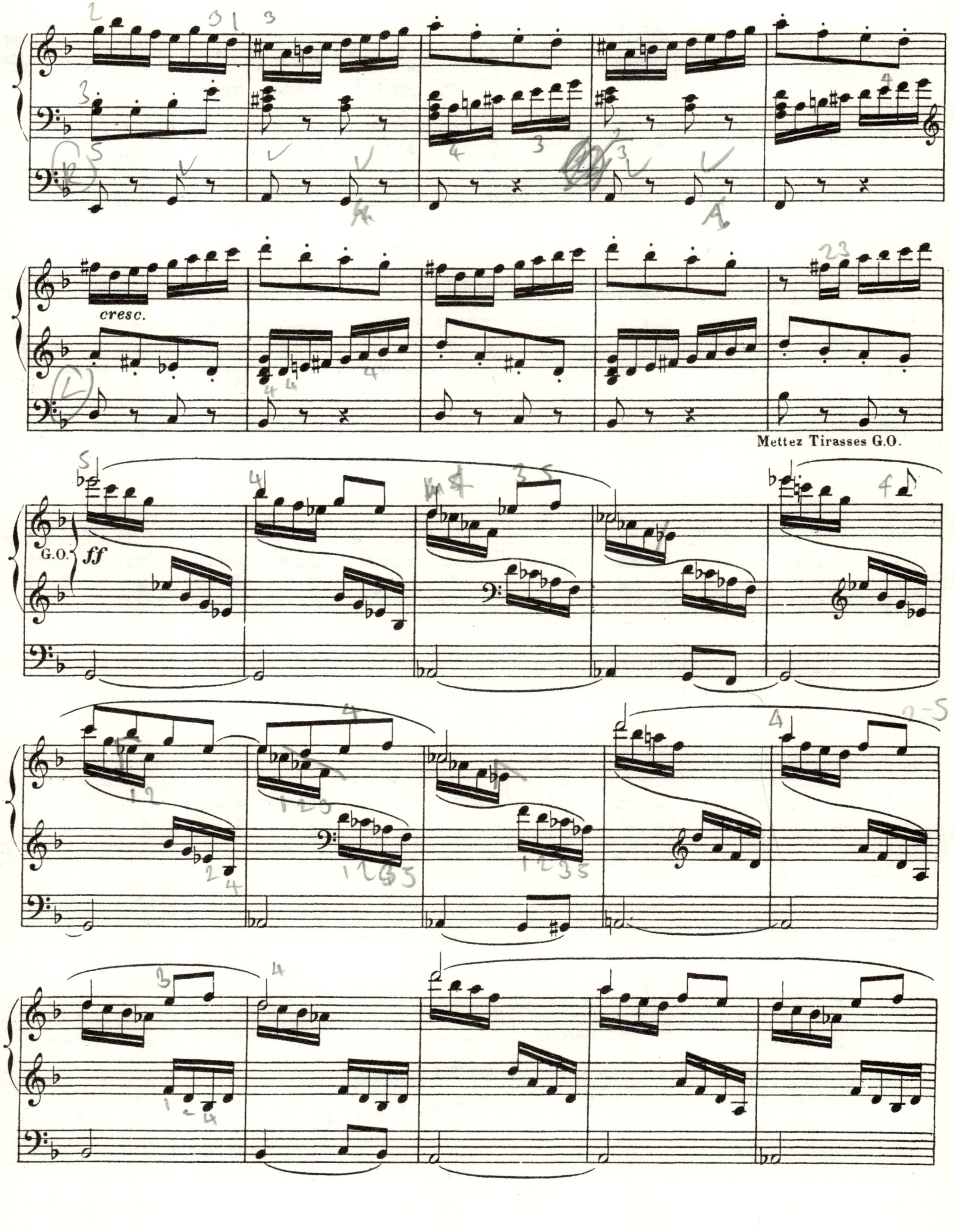
cresc.
Mettez Tirasses G.O.
G.O.
ff

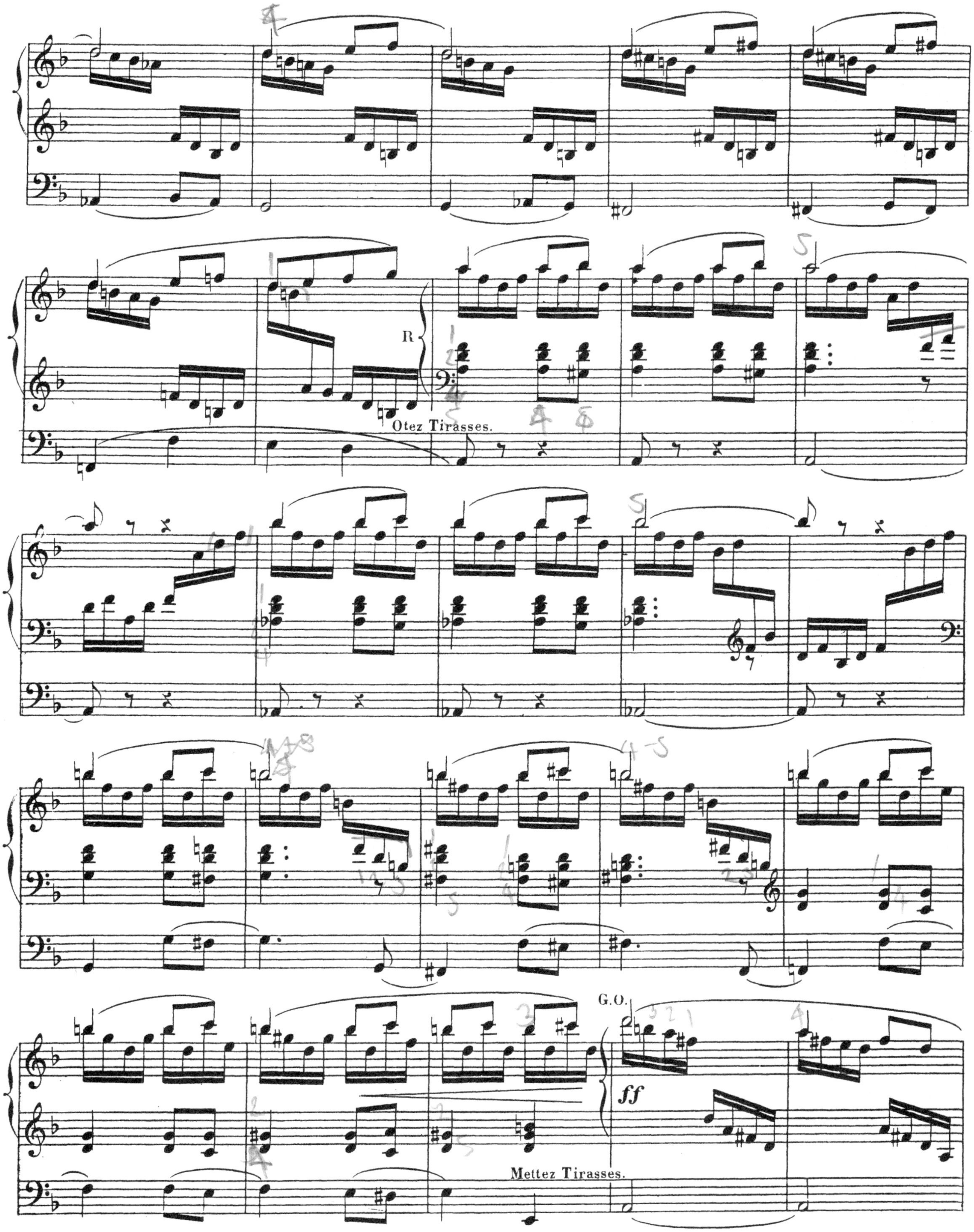
R
Otez Tirasses.
G.O.
ff
Mettez Tirasses.

100 / Renaud

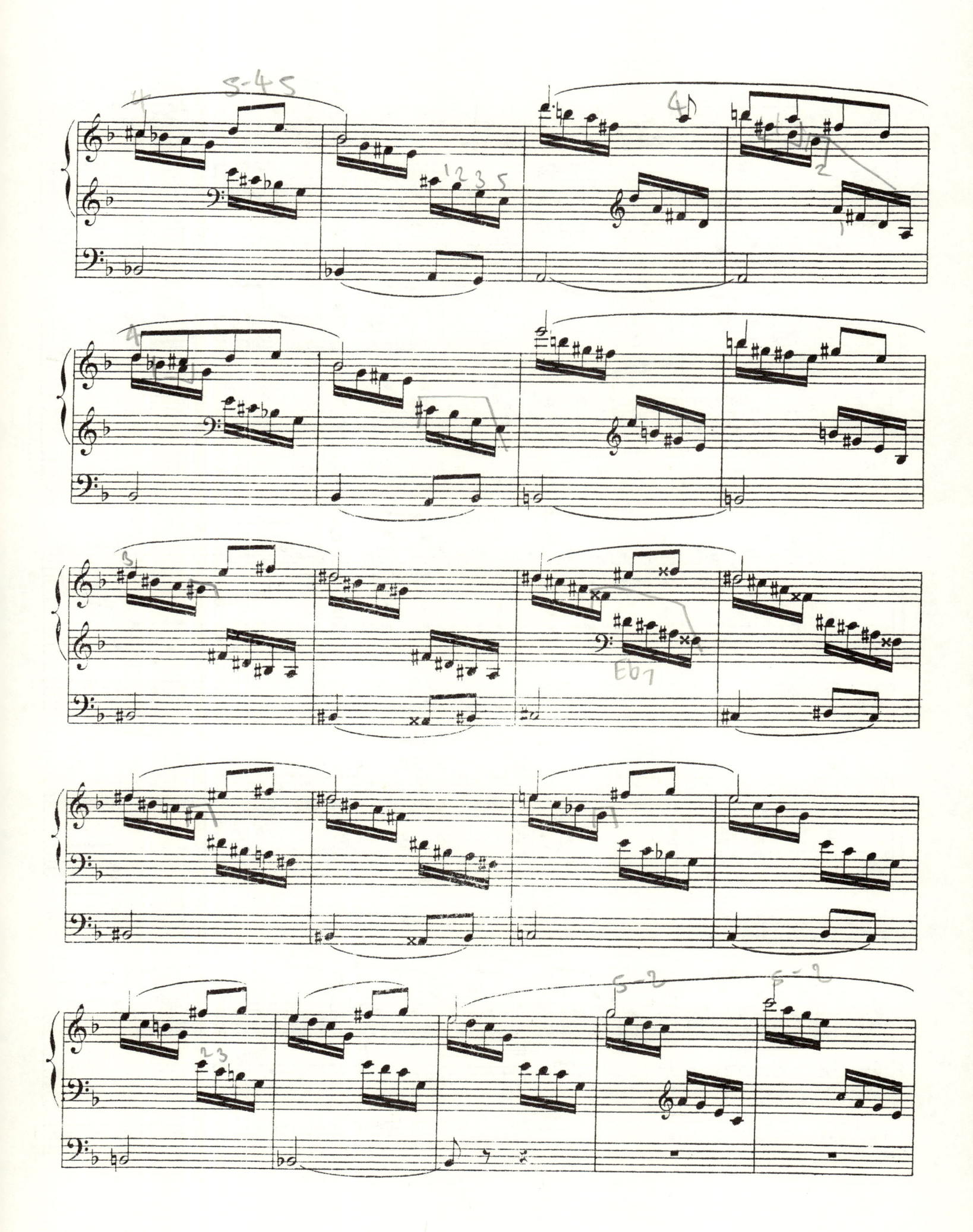

Renaud / 101

Otez Tirasses

G.O. sans les Anches (Récit accouplé)
Anches du G.O.
f
Mettez Tirasses

104 / Renaud

Al Chmo Maestro G. Ciocci

TOCCATA

III. (Recitativo) Fondi 8 e 4 ance e ripieni
II. (Positivo) Bordone e Salicionale 8
I. (Grand'Organo) Fondi 8 e 4
   3 manuali accopp.
Pedale 16 e 8

Remigio Renzi
1857–1938

106 / Renzi

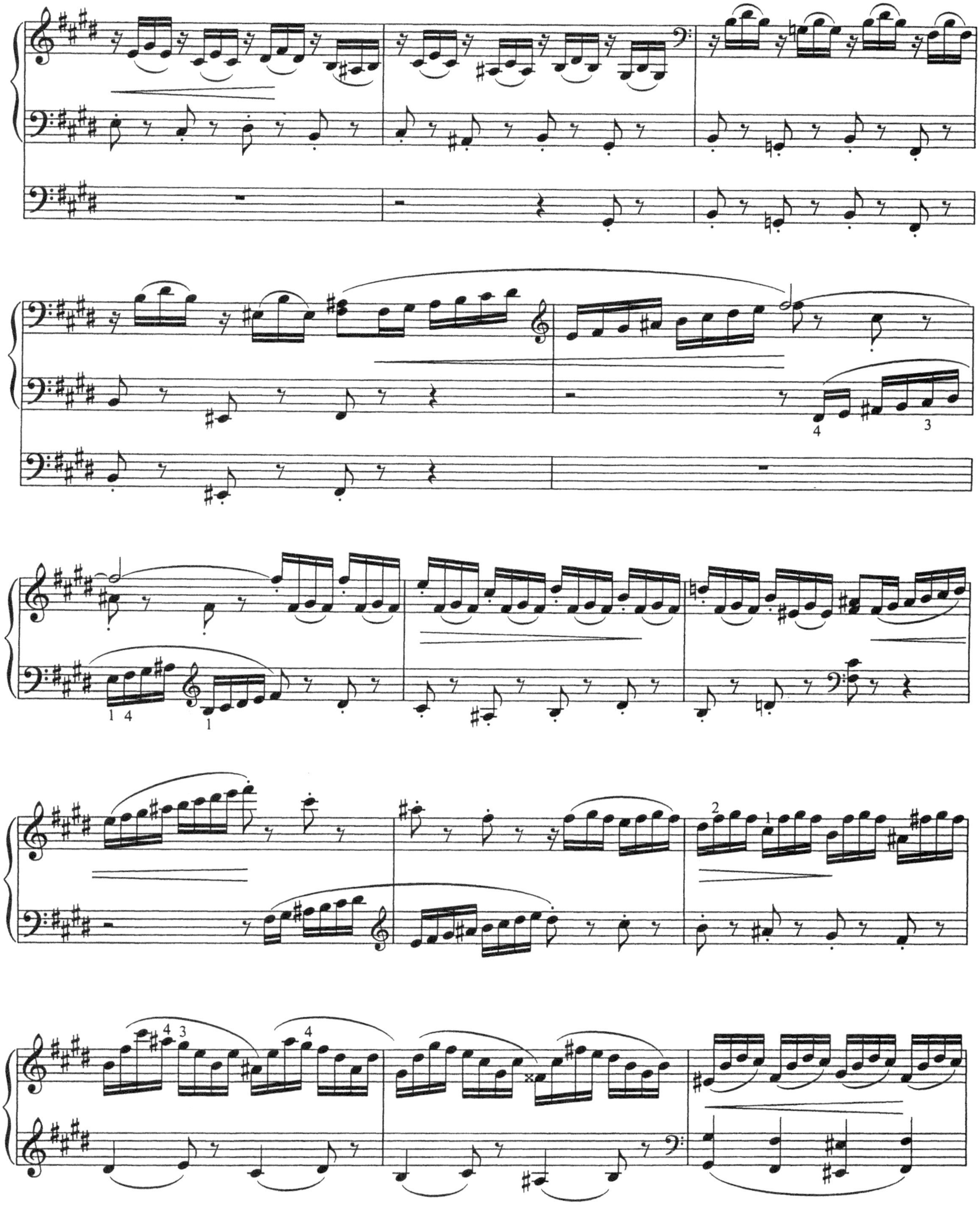

108 / Renzi

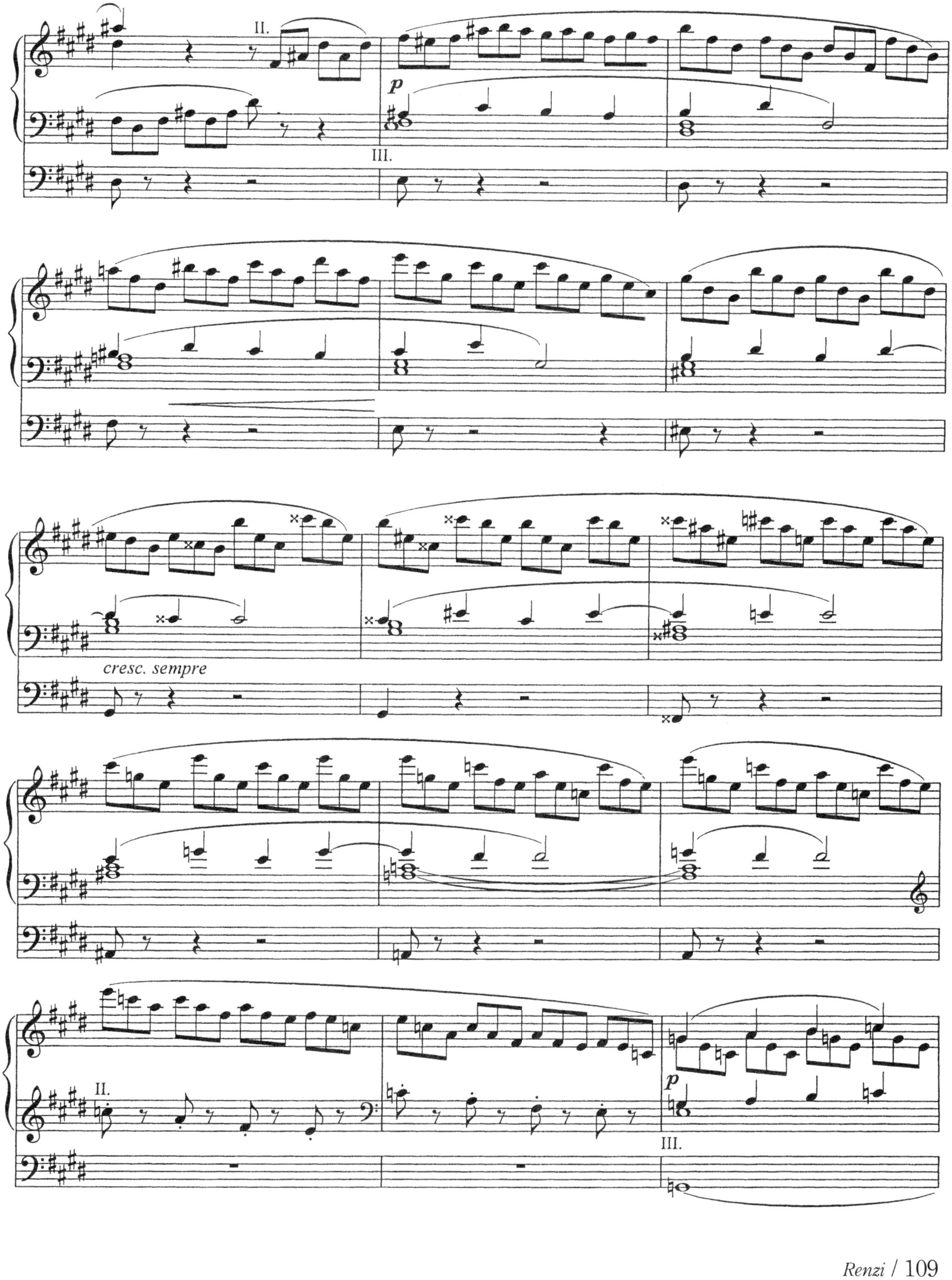
II.
p
III.
cresc. sempre
II.
p
III.

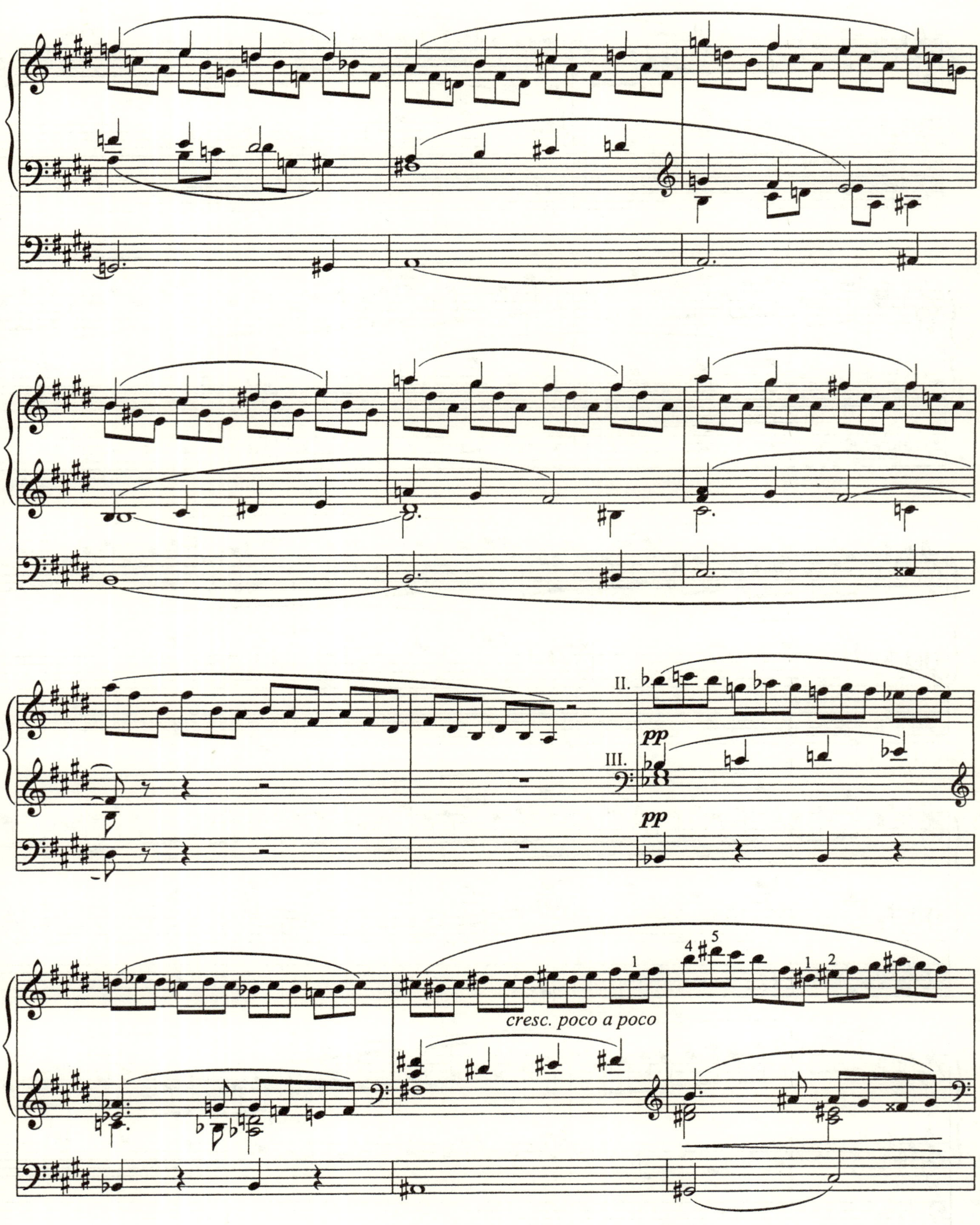
II.
III.
pp
pp
cresc. poco a poco

f
III. to I.
+4'
I.
All manuals coupled.
Add reeds and mixtures to III.
Tempo I.
III. opened
sempre staccato
I. to Ped.

112 / Renzi

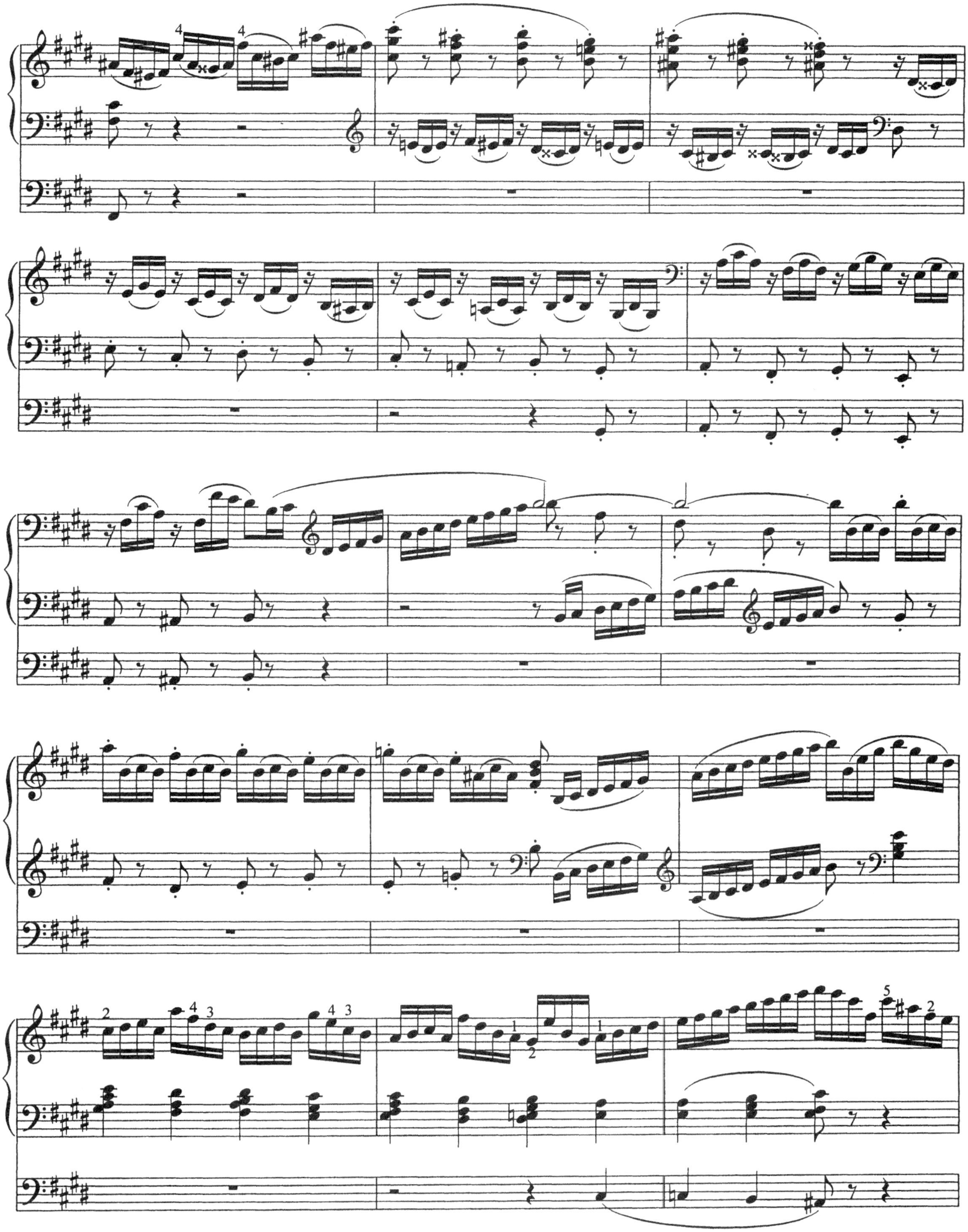

114 / Renzi

Fanfare d'Orgue
Étude de Concert

Full organ without heavy reeds and mixtures.

Harry Rowe Shelley
1858–1947

116 / Shelley

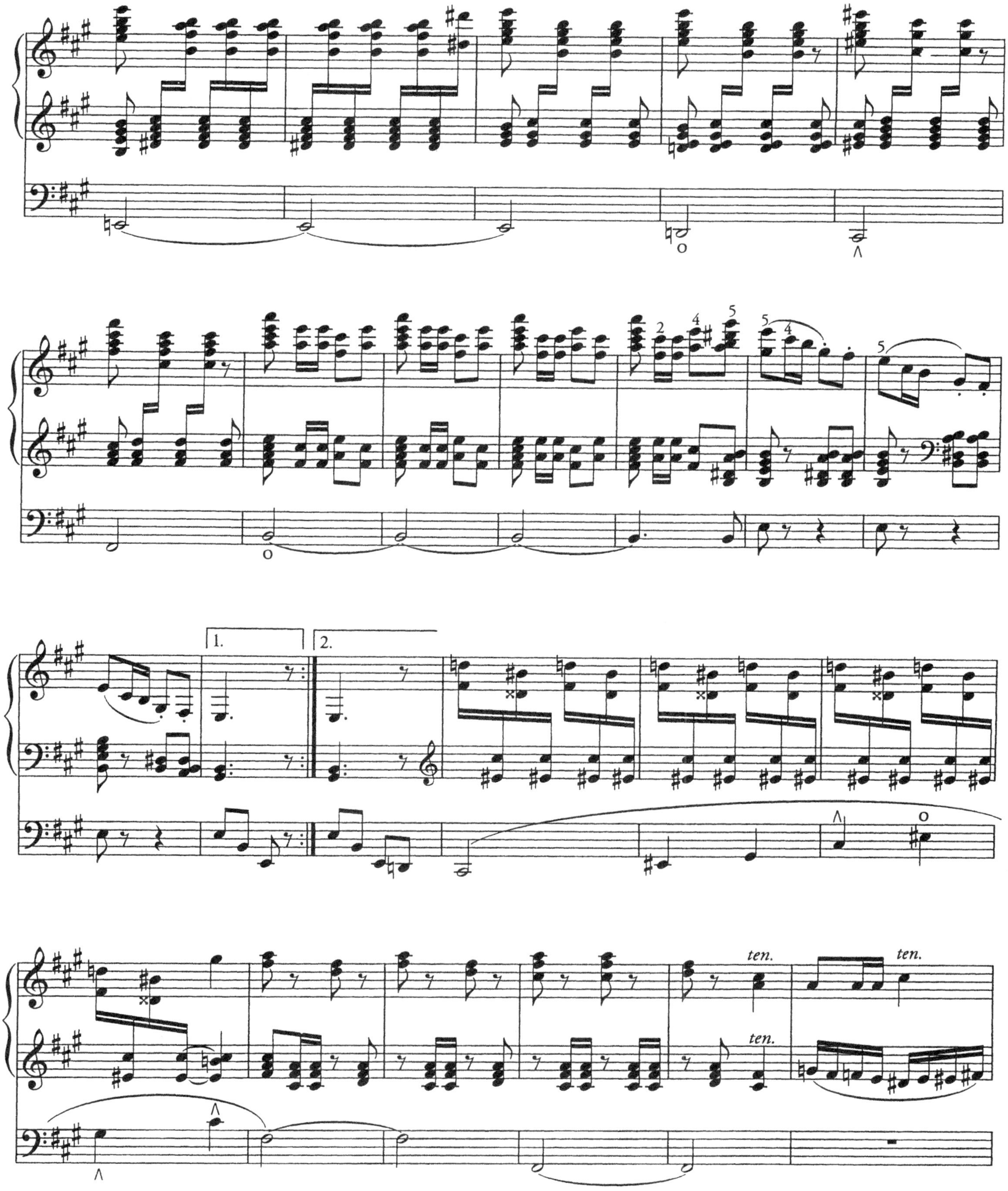
1.
2.
ten.
ten.
ten.

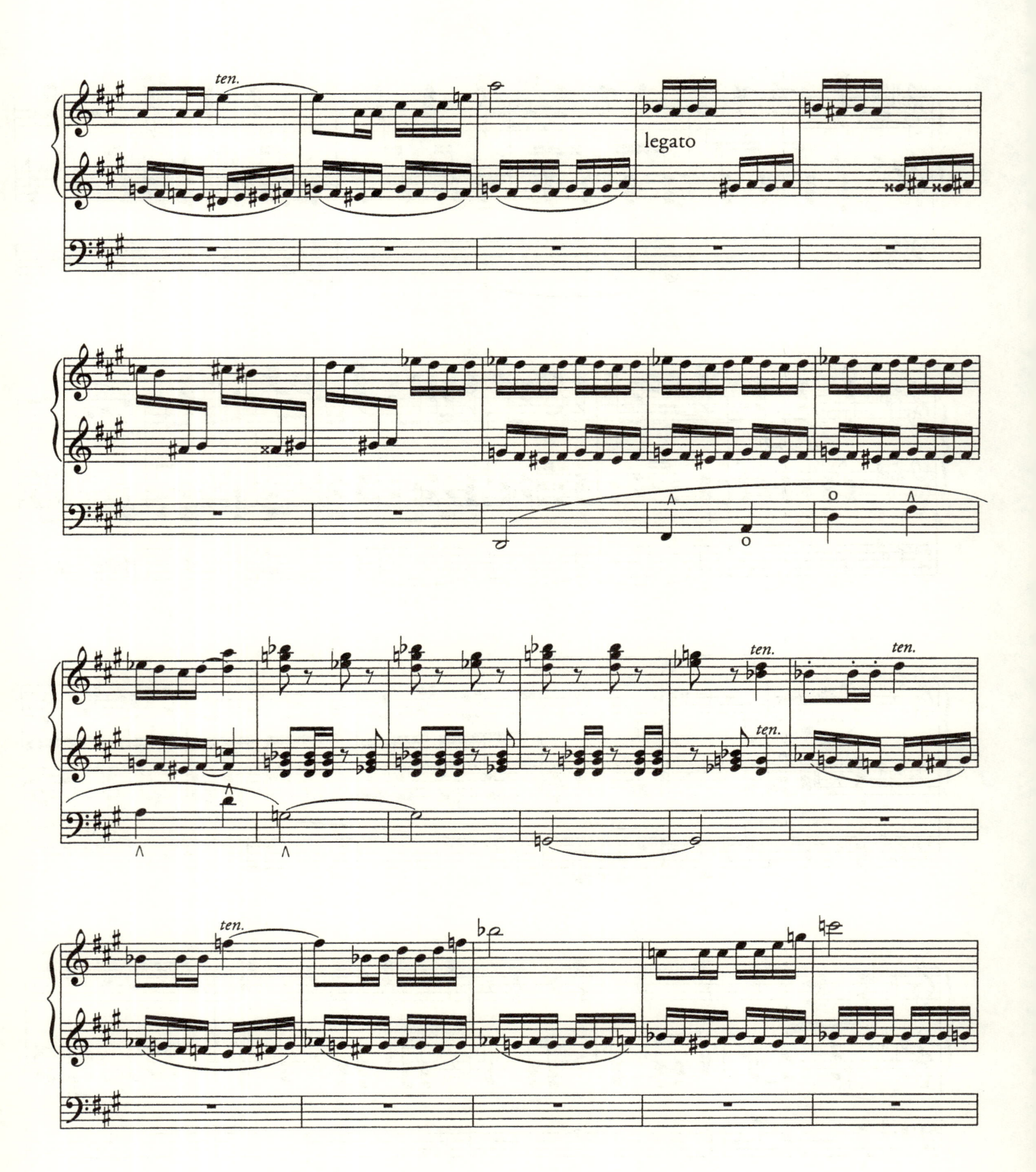
ten.
legato
ten.
ten.
ten.
ten.

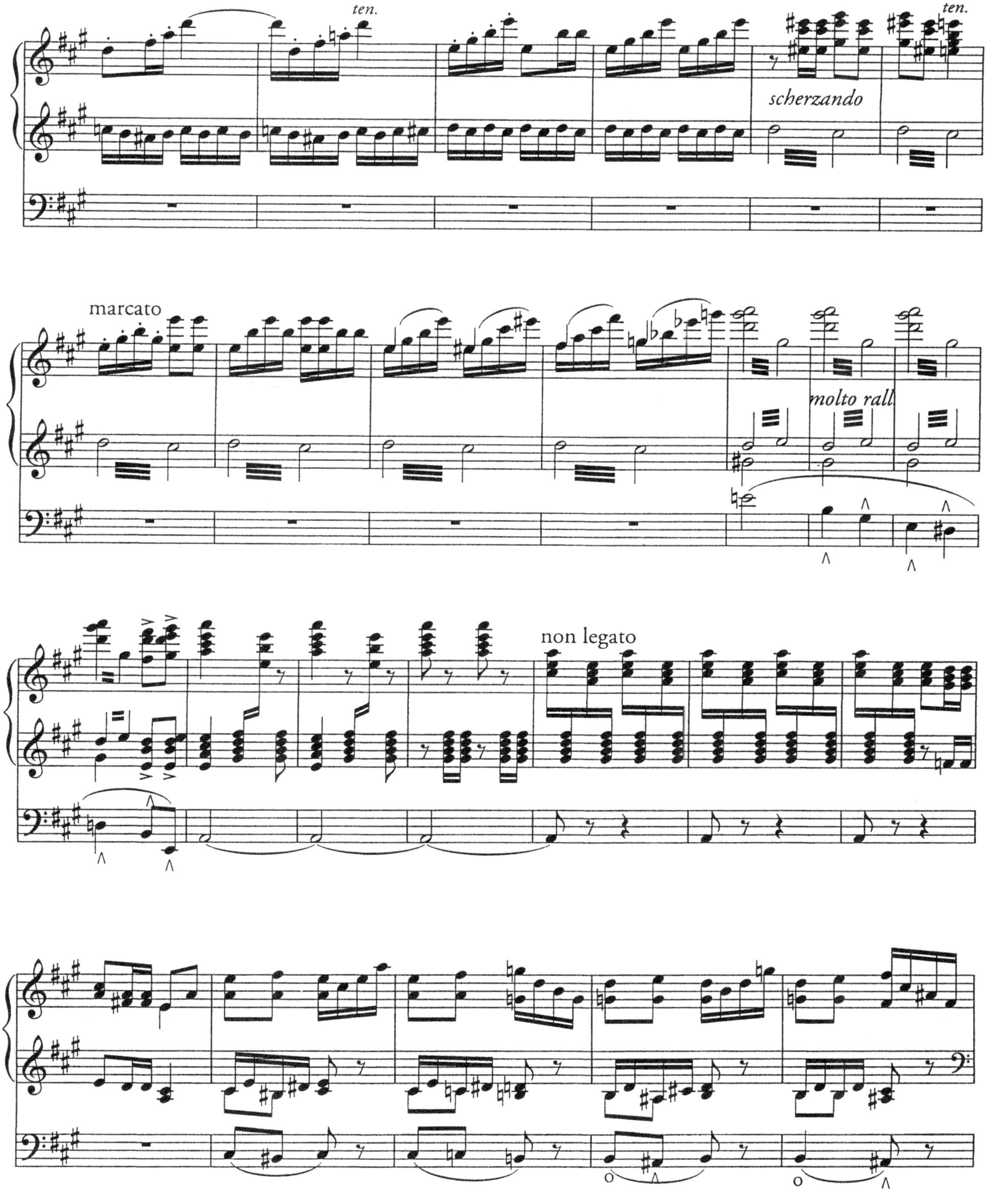
ten.
ten.
scherzando
marcato
molto rall.
non legato

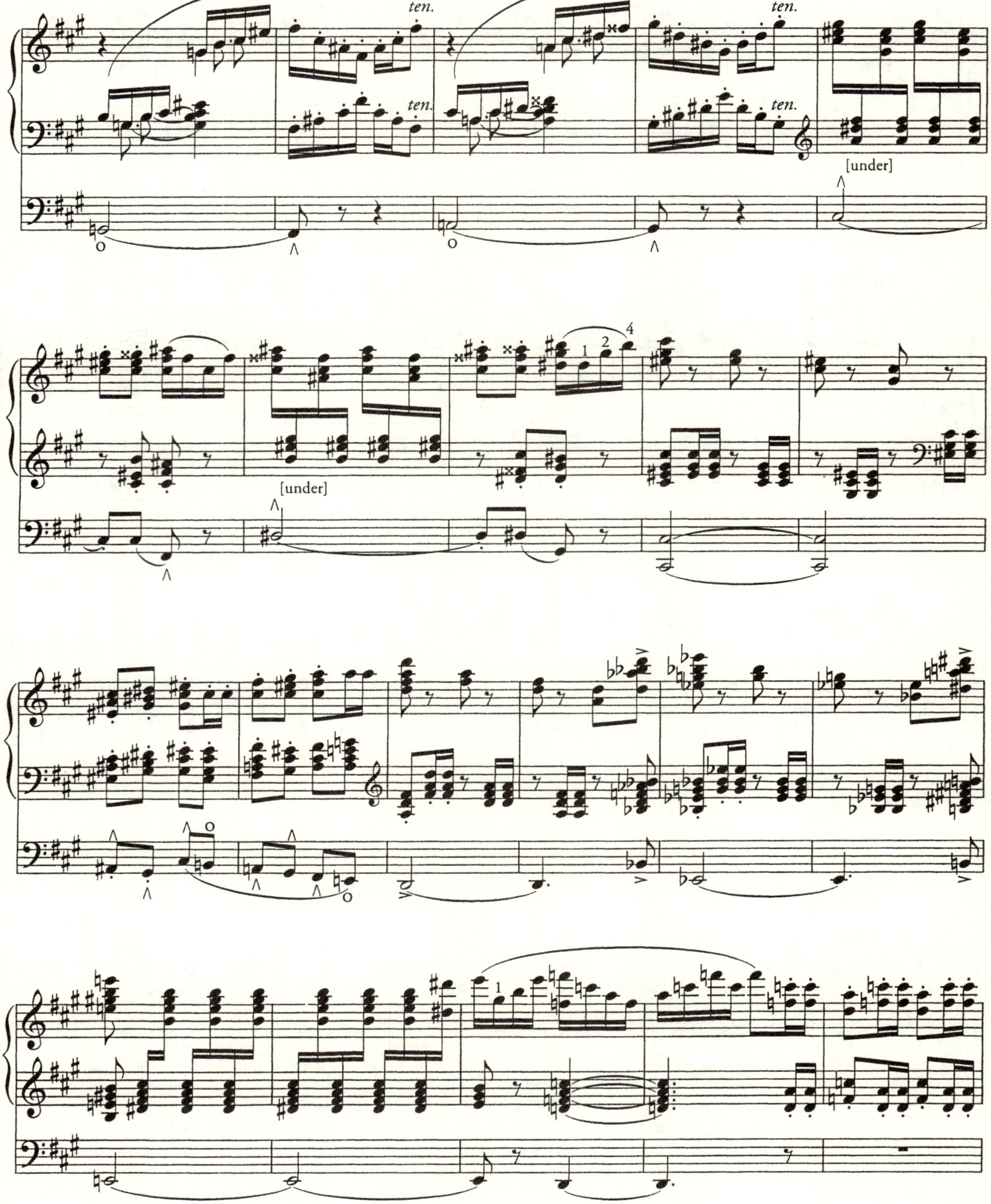
ten.
ten.
ten.
ten.
[under]
[under]

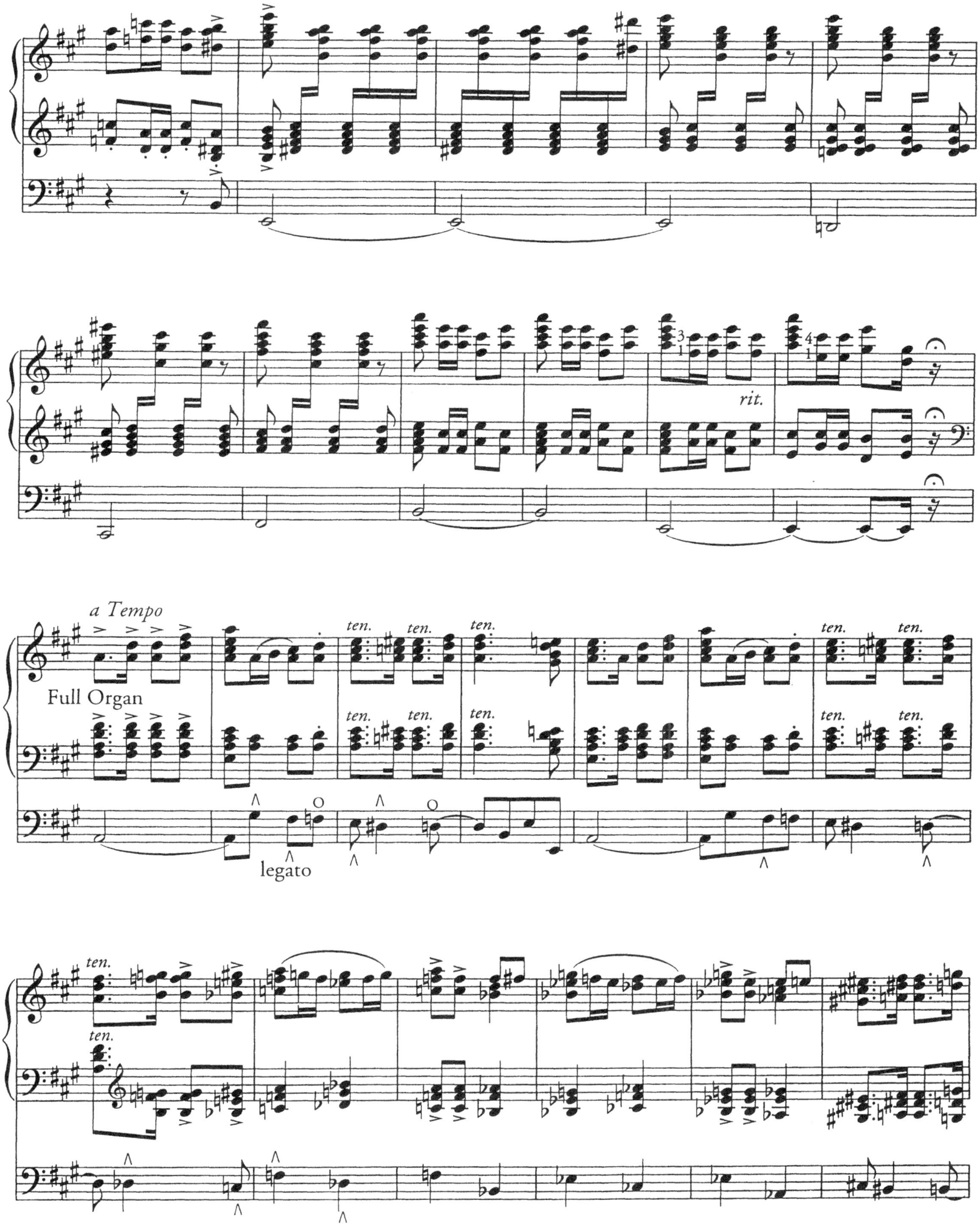
rit.
a Tempo
Full Organ
ten.
legato

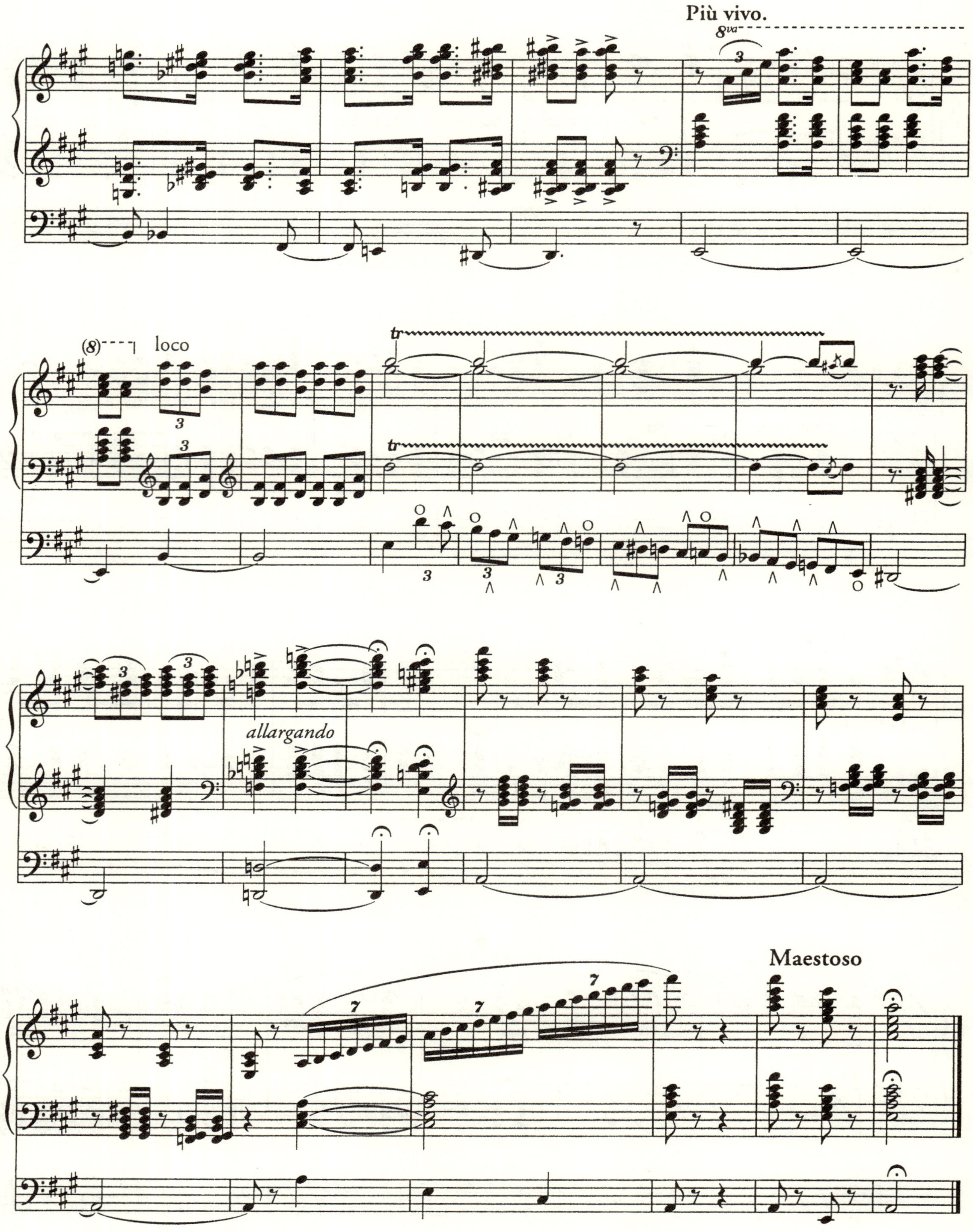
Più vivo.
8va
(8)
loco
tr
allargando
Maestoso

à Ferdinand de la Tombelle

TOCCATA
Op. 19, No. 3

G.P.R. Fonds et Anches 8 et 4
Péd. Fonds et Anches 16 et 8
Claviers accouplés

Charles Tournemire
1870–1939

124 / Tournemire

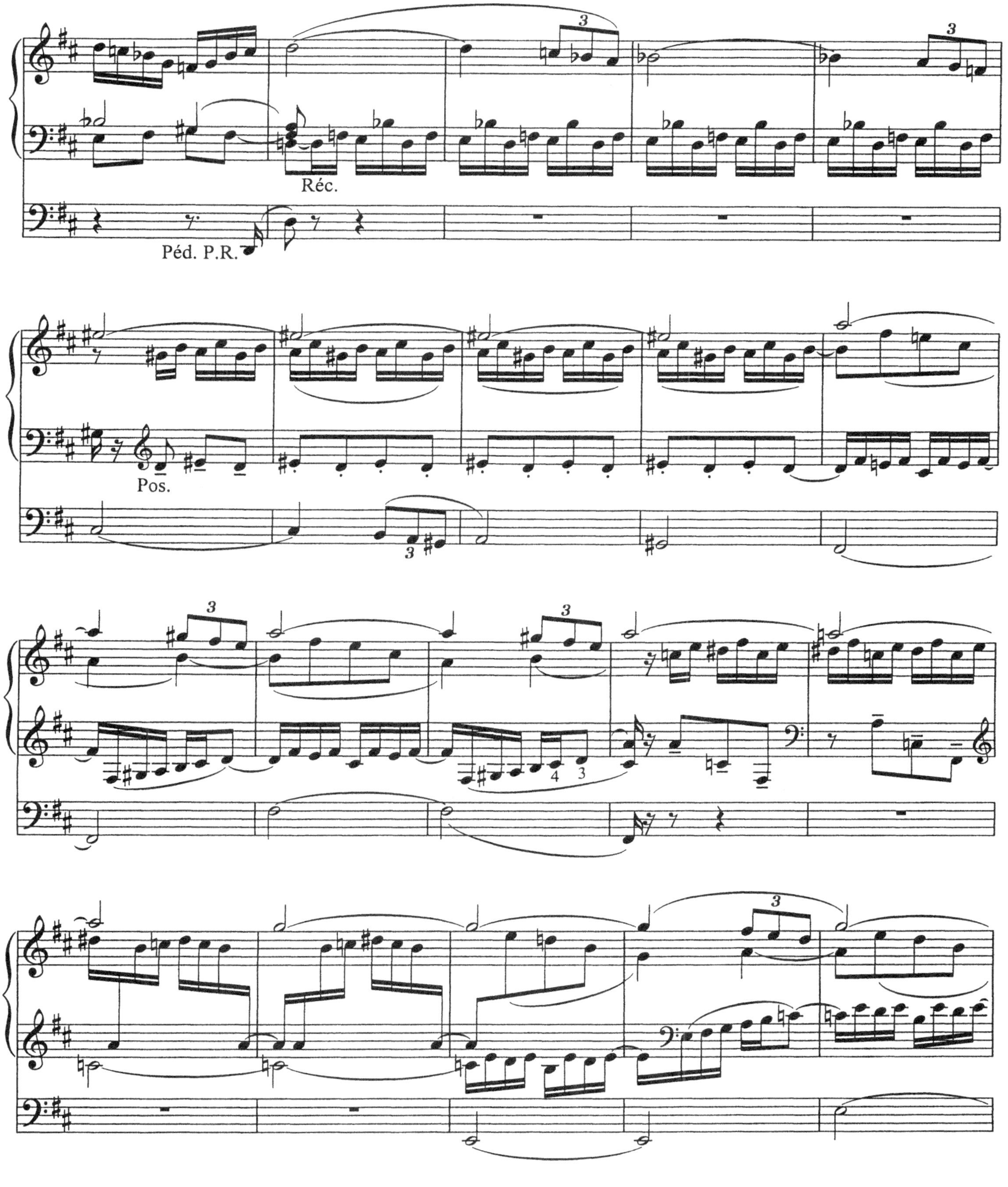
Réc.
Péd. P.R.
Pos.

126 / Tournemire

Rall.
Un poco largamente
Rall.
fff
G.P.R.
Octaves ad lib.
Pédale Anches 16' 8' 4'

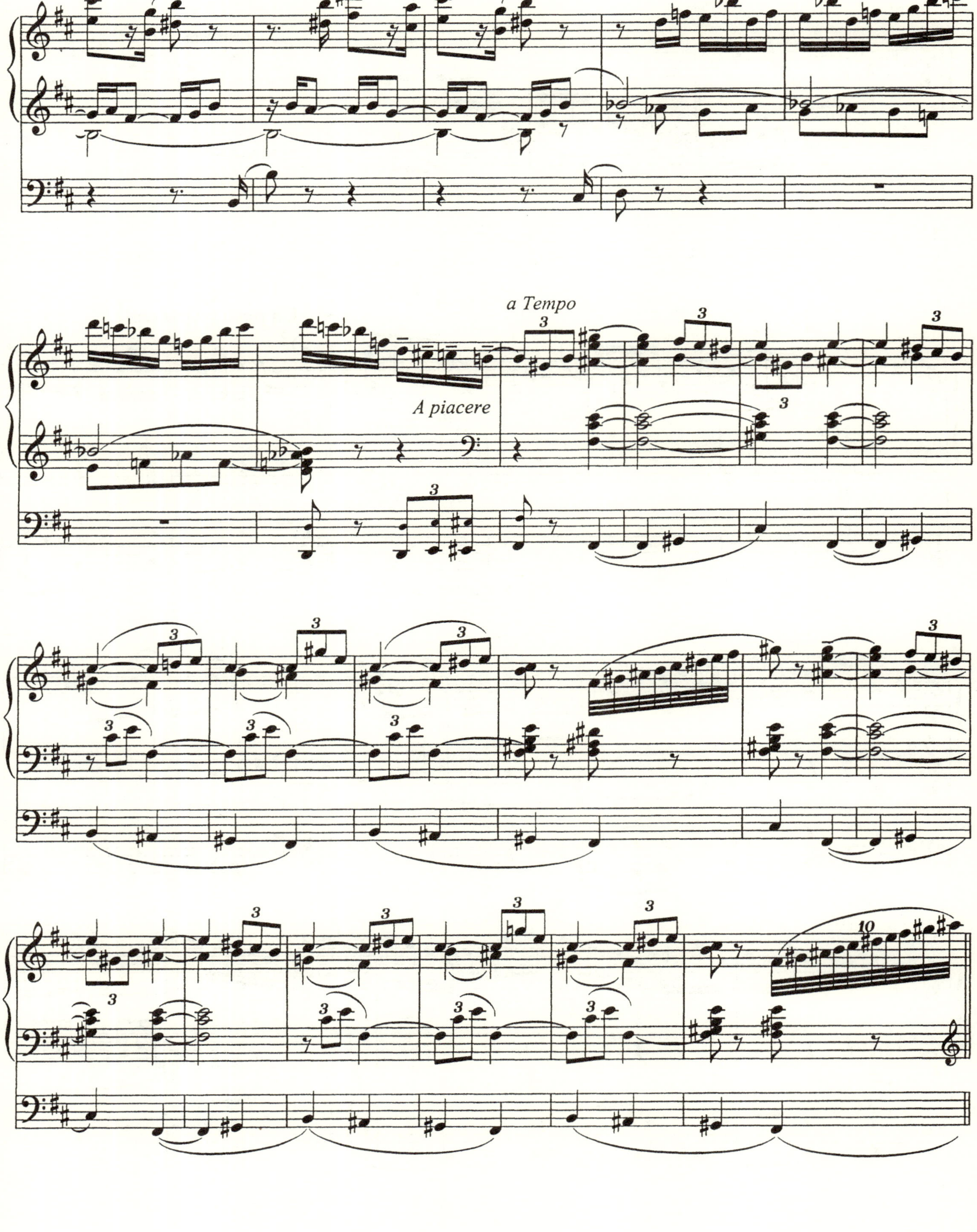
a Tempo
A piacere

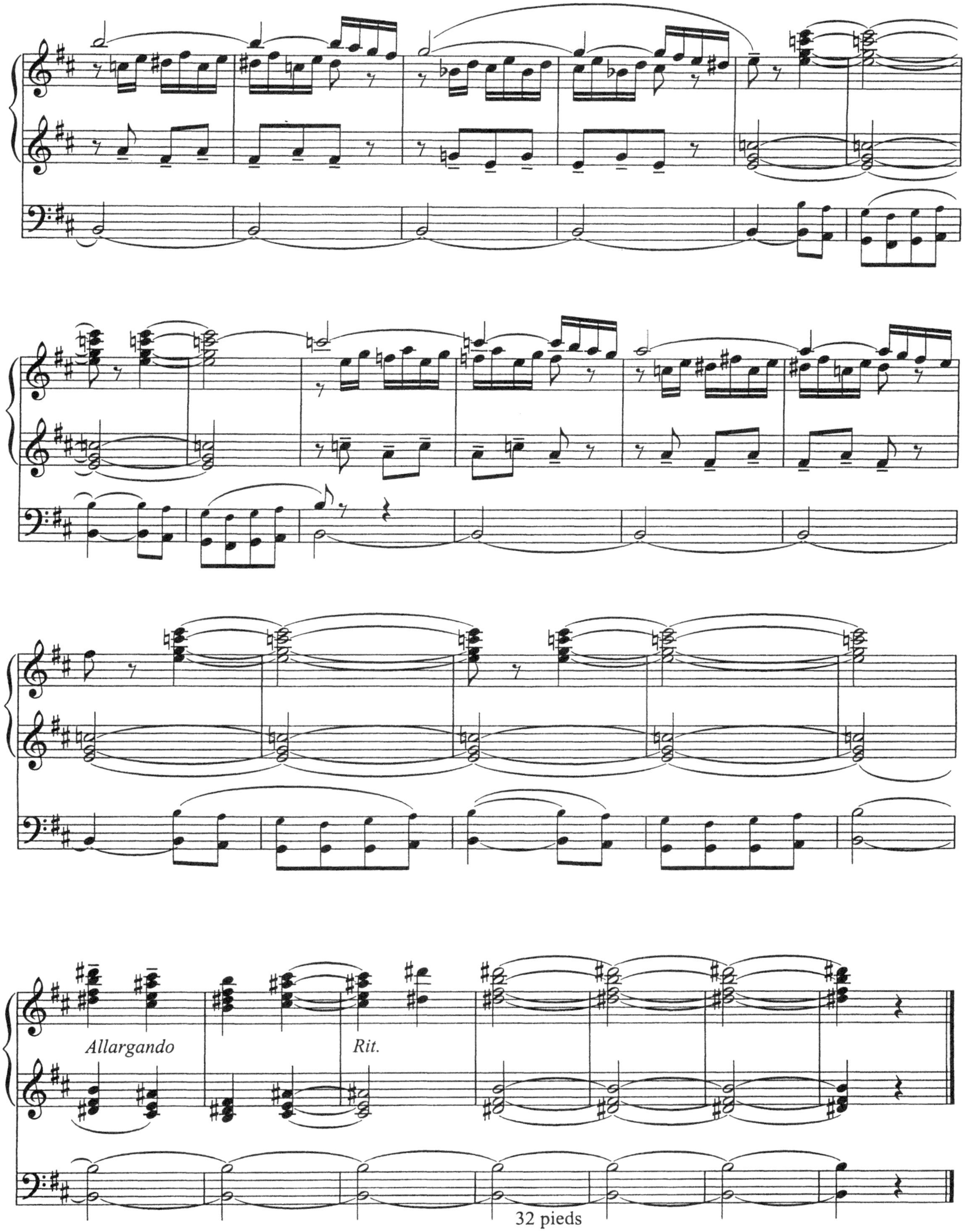
Allargando
Rit.
32 pieds

TOCCATA

Charles-Marie Widor
1844–1937

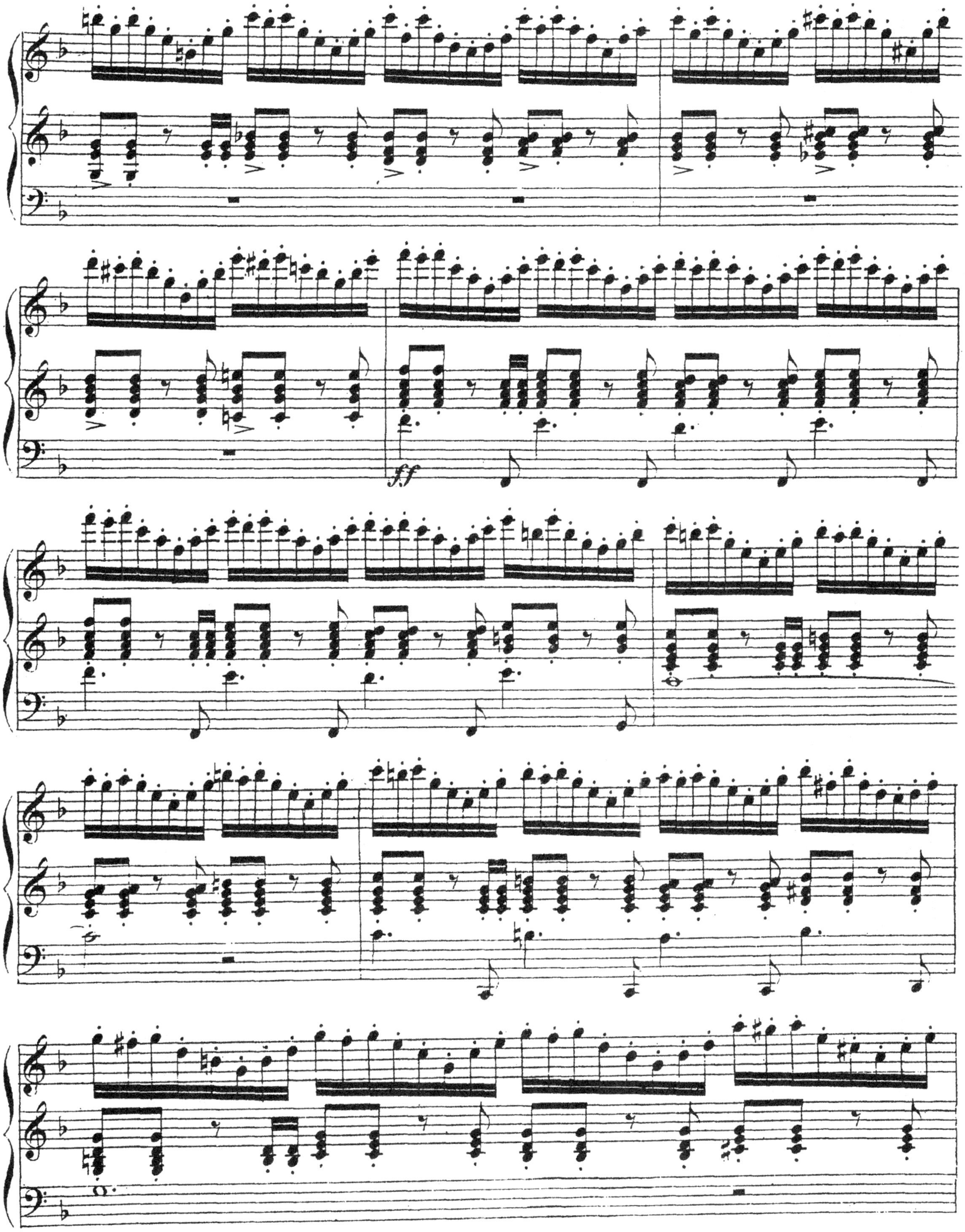
ff

132 / Widor

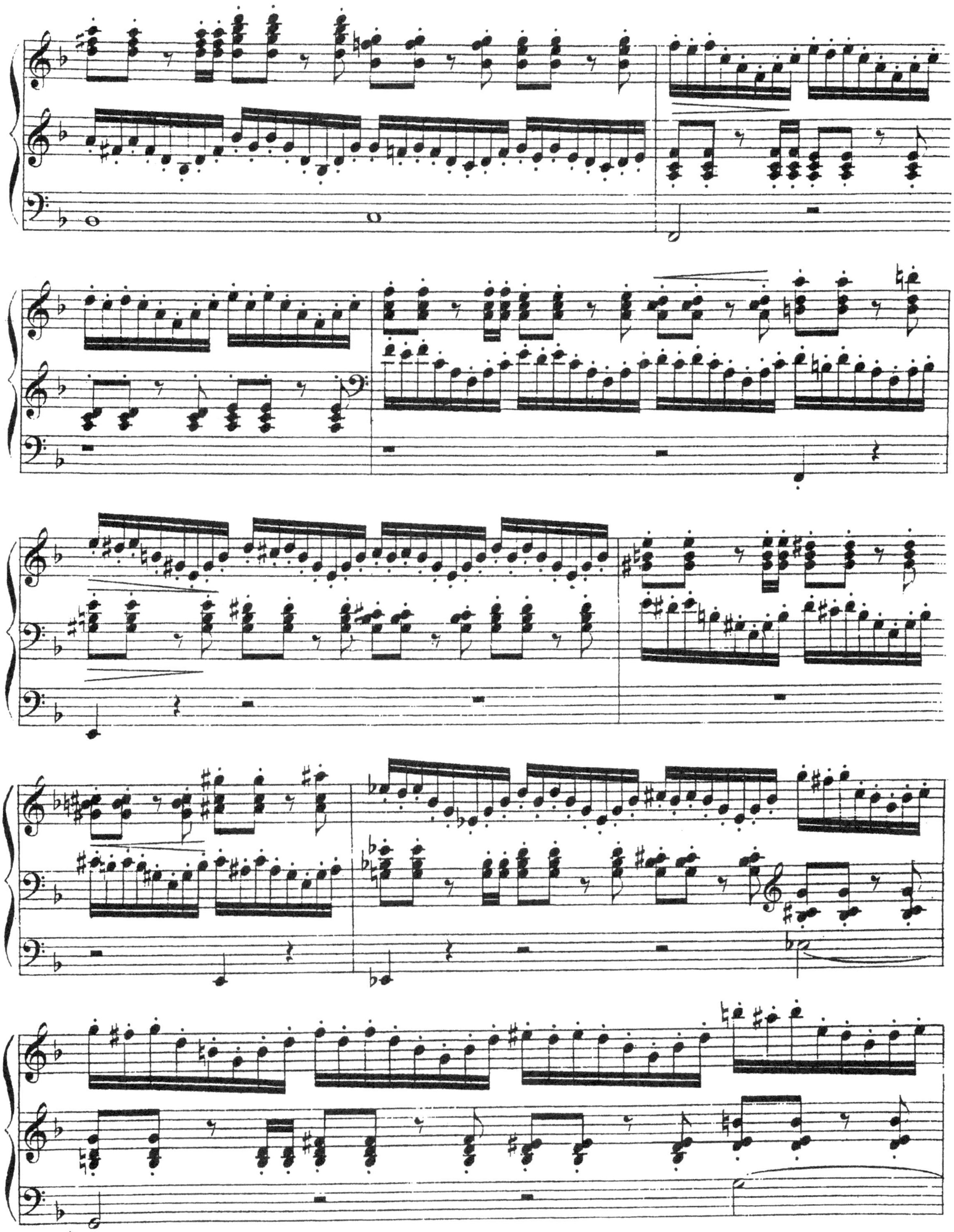

134 / Widor

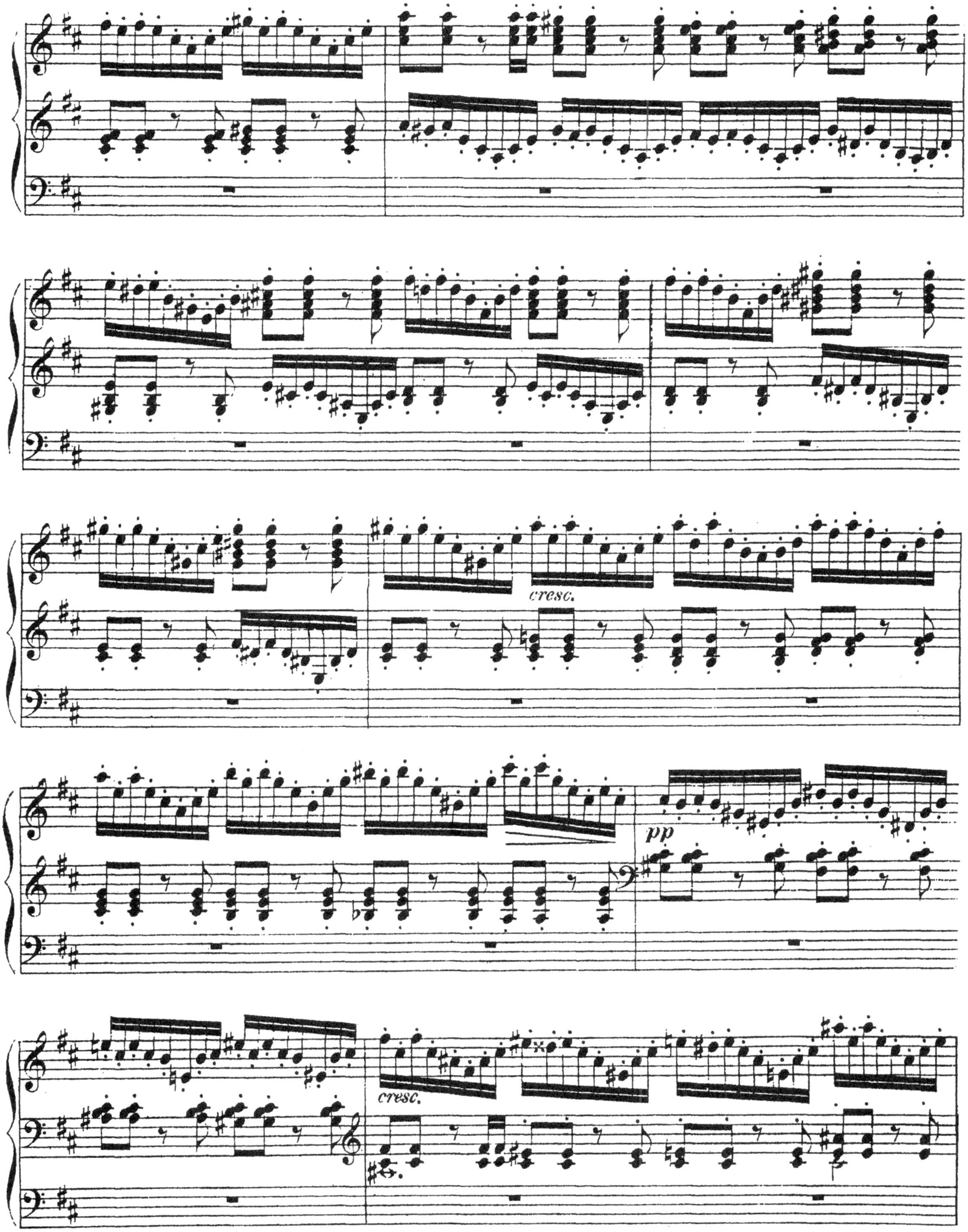
cresc.
pp
cresc.

136 / Widor

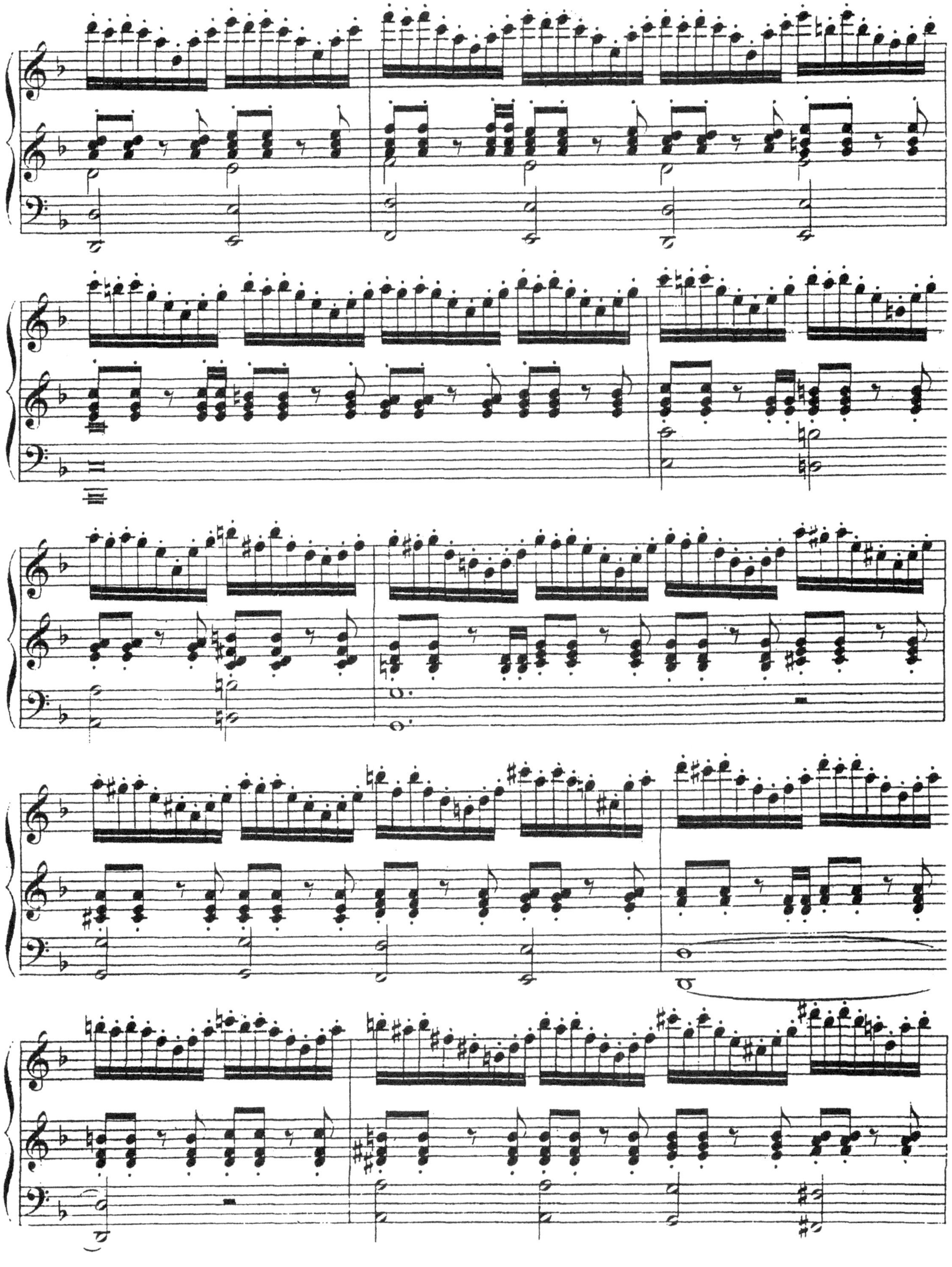

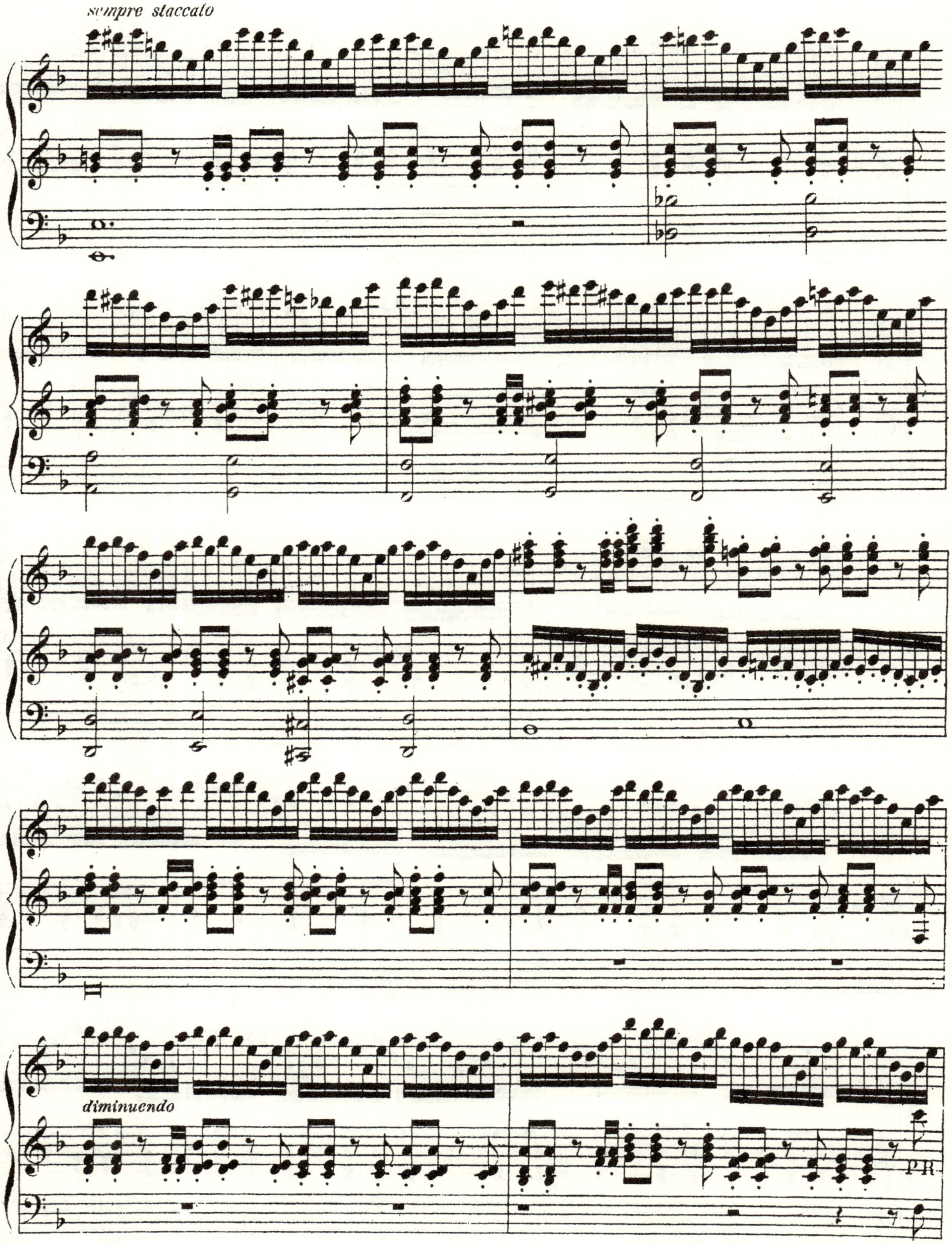
sempre staccato
diminuendo
PR

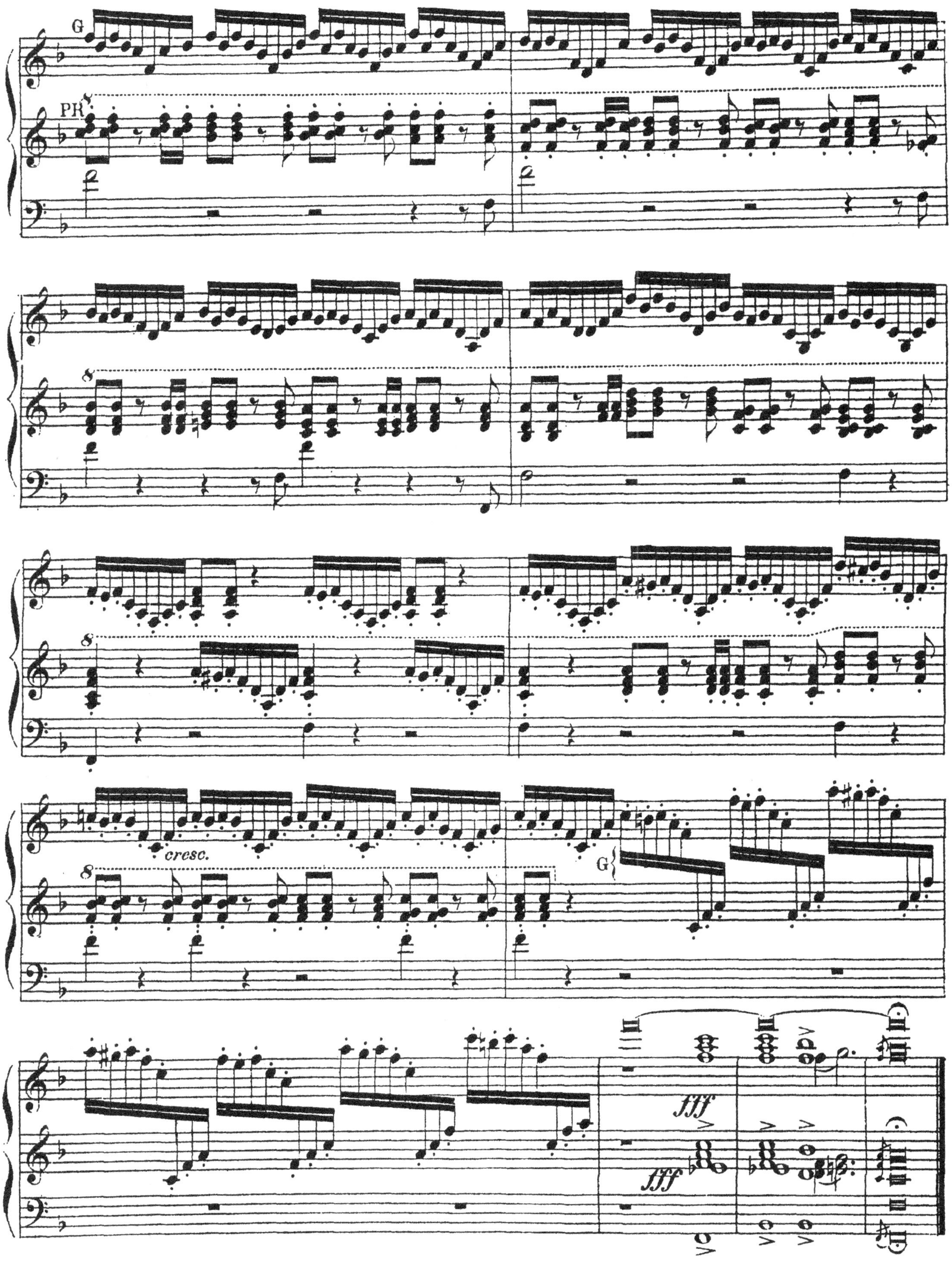
G
PR
cresc.
G
fff
fff

To Clarence Dickinson

Humoresque "L'organo primitivo"
Toccatina for Flute

Manual: One Flute 8'
Pedal: Bourdon 16'
      Manual to Pedal

Pietro A. Yon
1886–1943

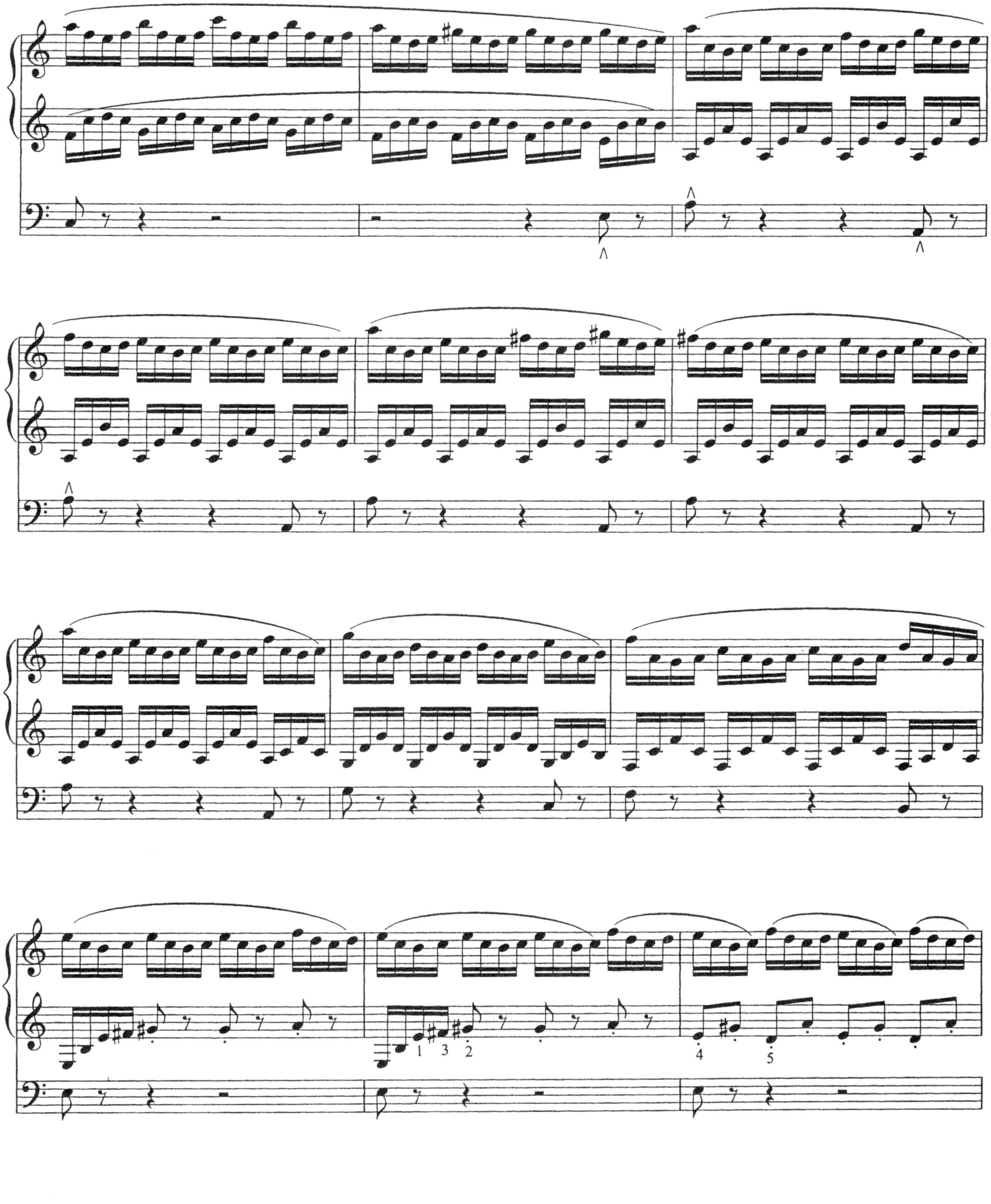
1
3
2
4
5

142 / Yon

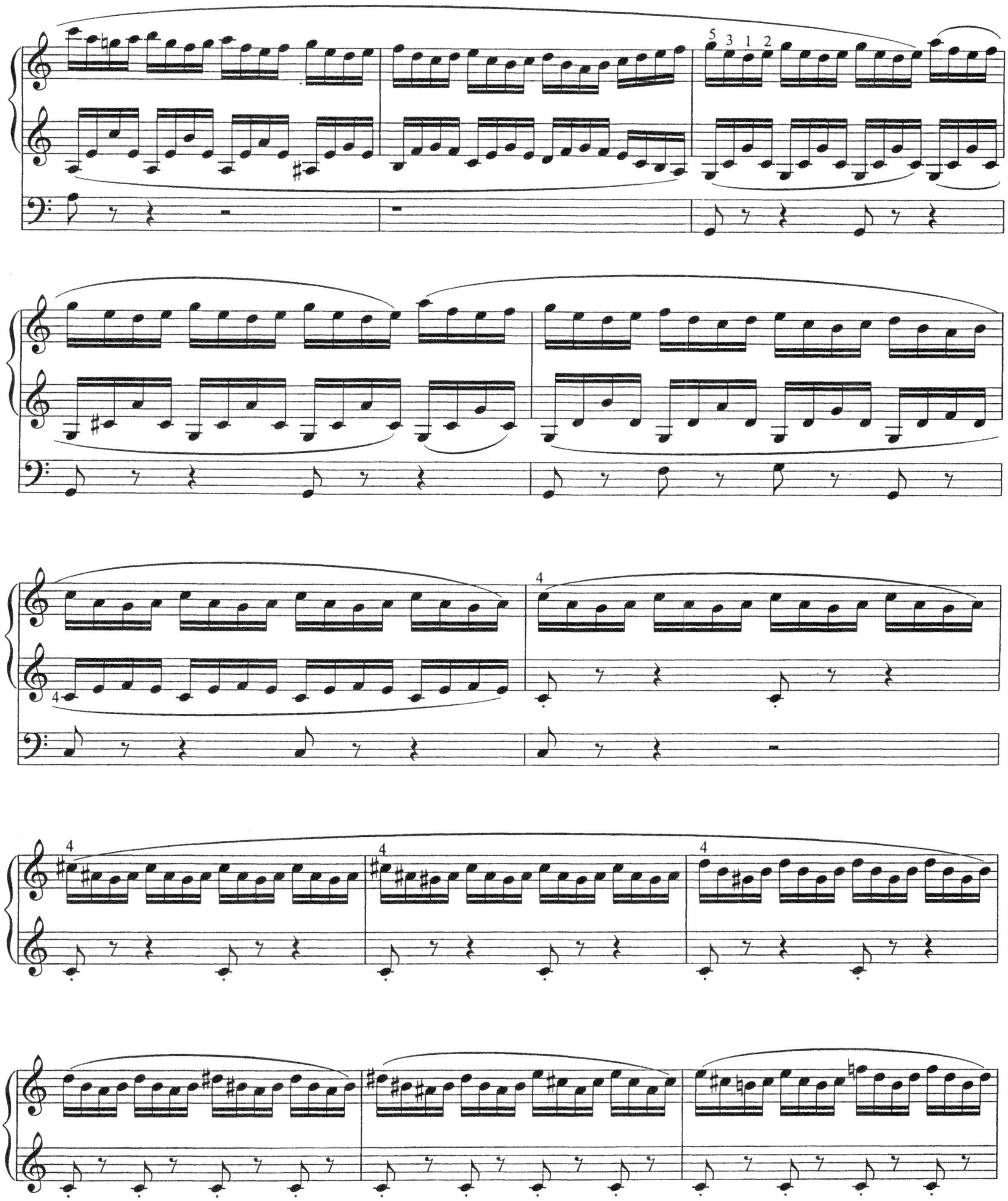

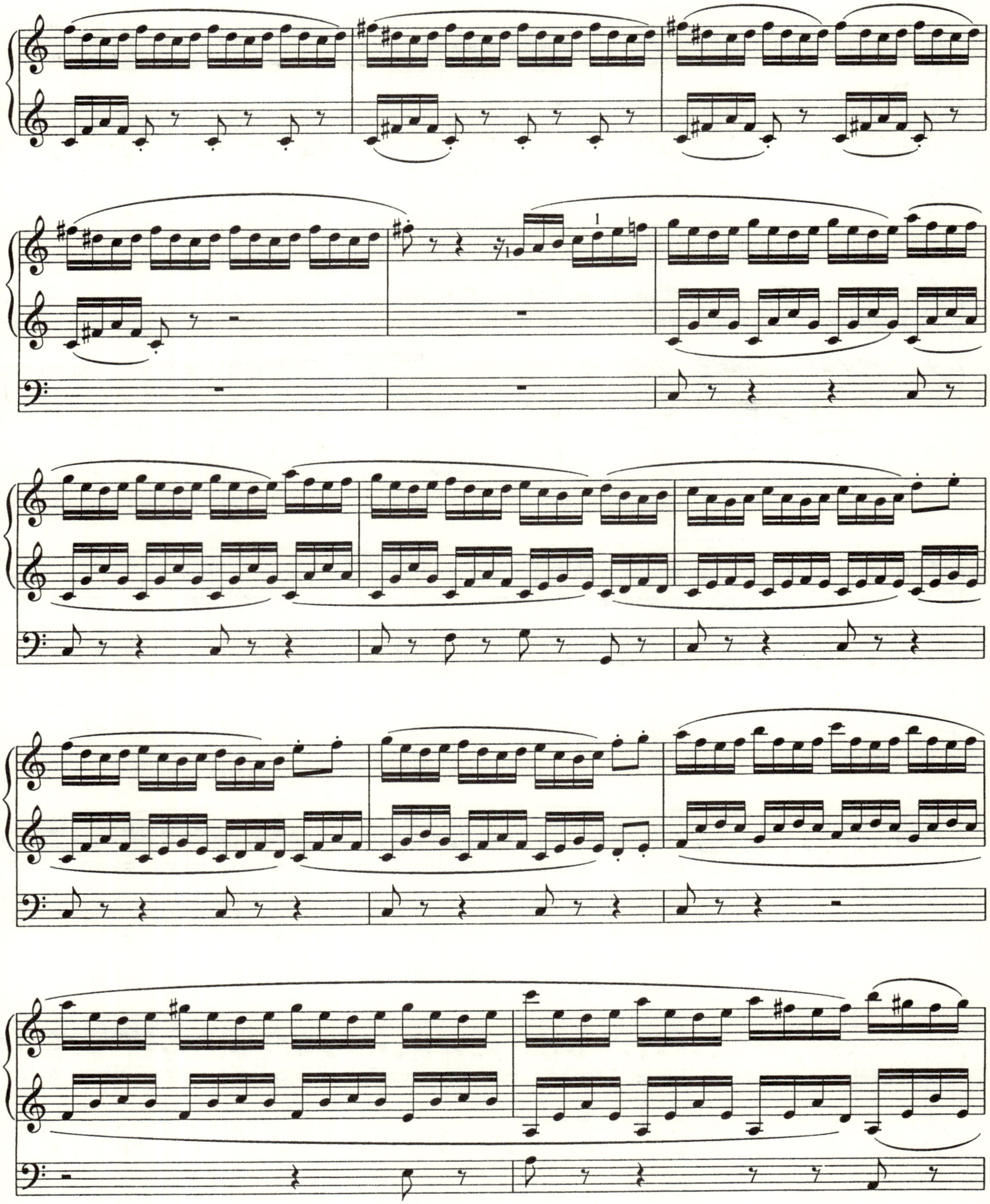

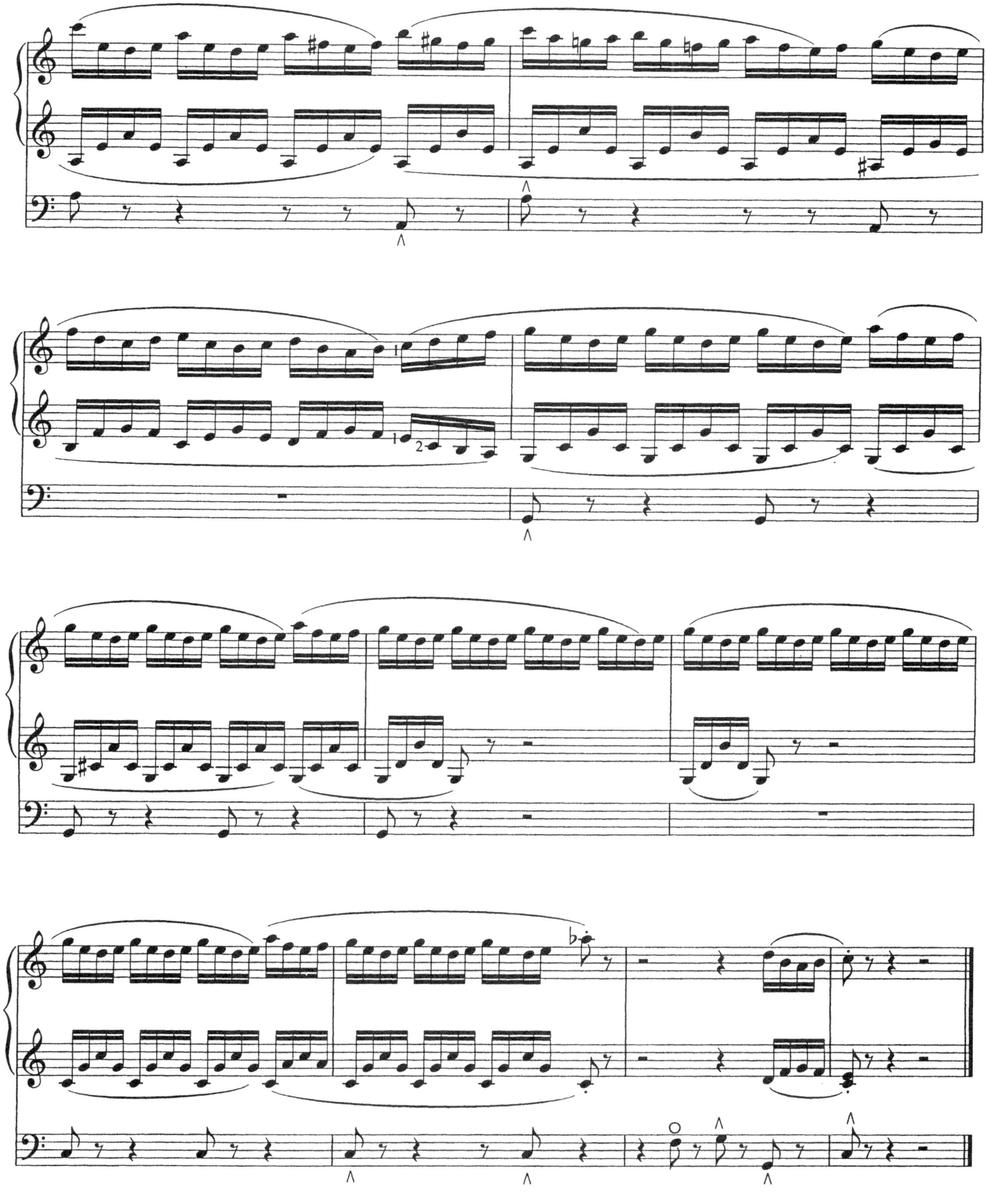

CARILLONS

À *Monsieur* TH. DUBOIS

CARILLON
Op. 16, No. 5

G^d Orgue. Grand Chœur (*ff*)
Récit. Fonds et Anches de 8 et 4 P.
Pédale. Fonds et Anches de 4, 8 et 16 P.

Léon Boëllmann
1862–1897

Boëllmann / 149

150 / Boëllmann

Récit.
p
Gd O.
mf
Pos.
f
Accoup- du Récit.
Mettez les Anches du Pos.
Tirasse du Récit.
Pos.
Gd O. ff
Mettez les Anches de la Péd. et du Gd O.

152 / Boëllmann

à MARCEL DUPRÉ

CARILLONS
Op. 7, No. 2

Récit. Fonds 8, 4, Hautbois, Plein jeu.
Positif. Fonds 8, Tierce, Nazard.
G^d Orgue. Fonds 8, 4, Quinte
Pédale. 16, 8, 4.

Émile Bourdon
1884–1974

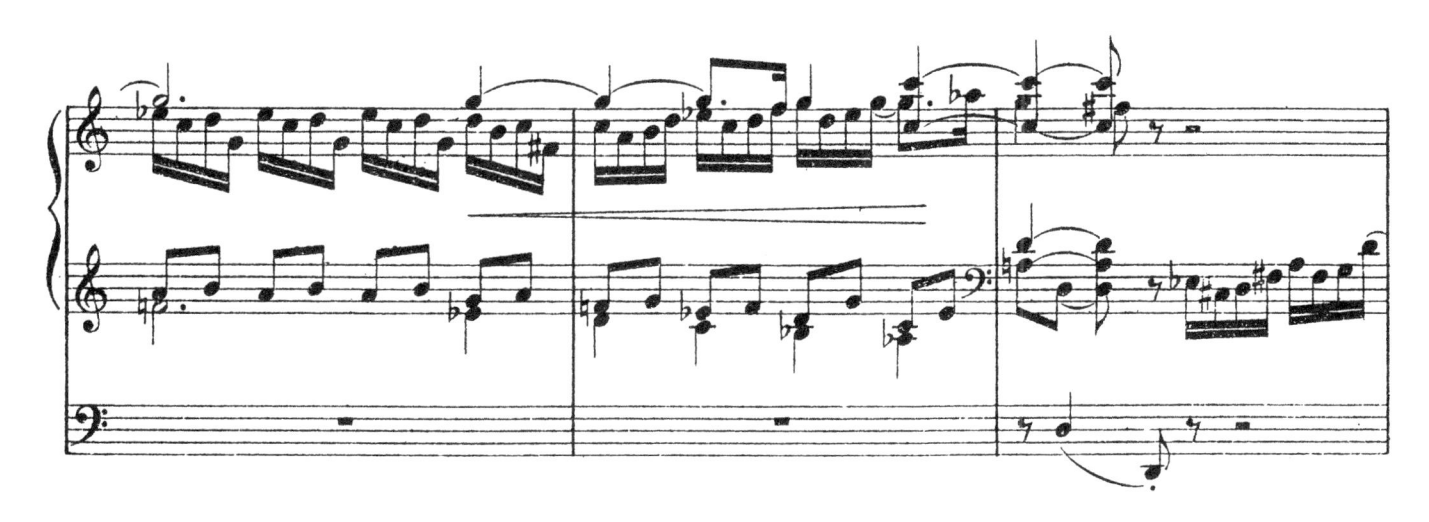

154 / *Bourdon*

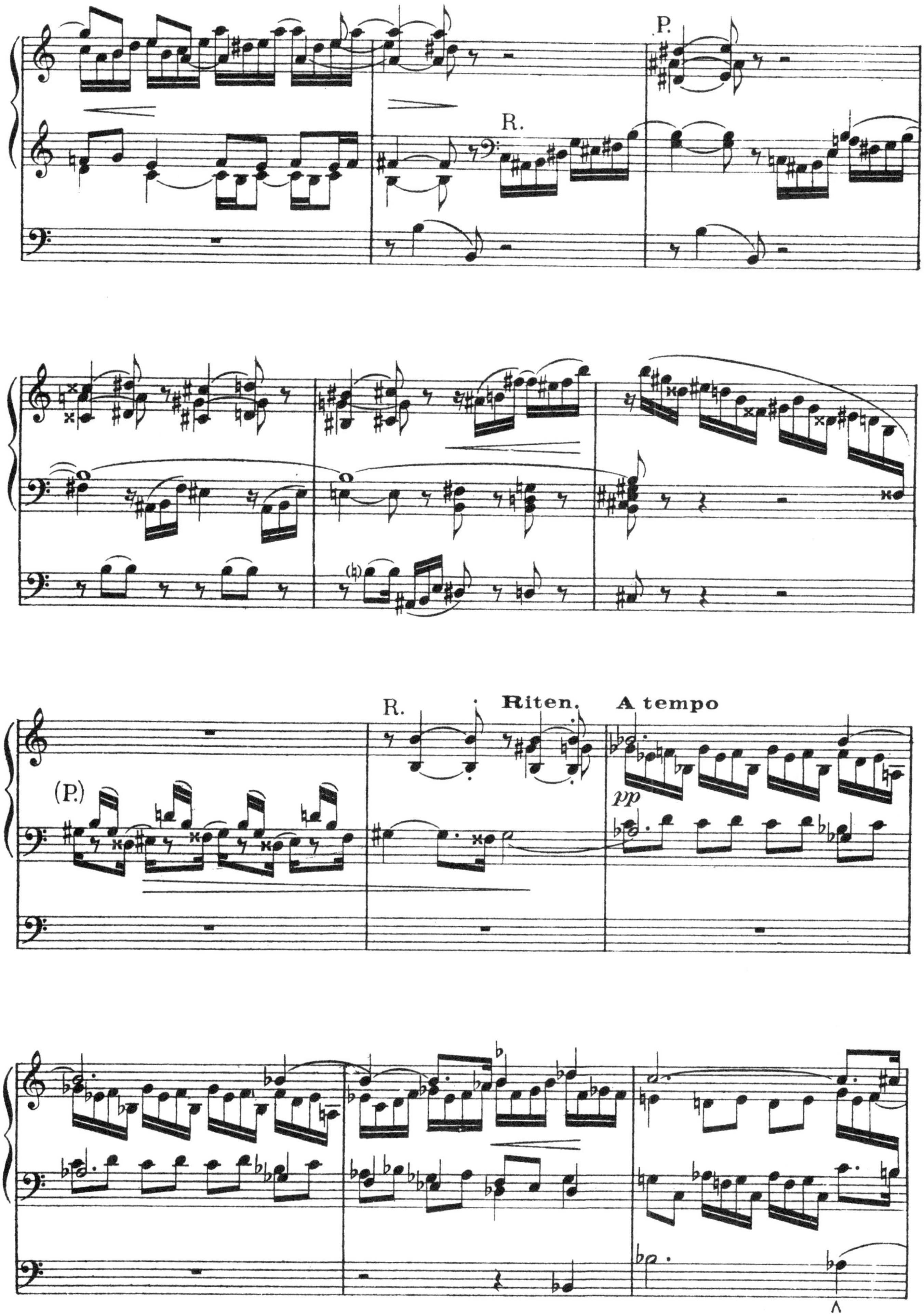
P.
R.
R.
Riten.
A tempo
(P.)
pp

156 / *Bourdon*

Bourdon / 157

158 / Bourdon

THE BELLS

The Mournful Bells of Reims

Prelude-Verset No. 6 for the Magnificat for the Feast of All Saints
(preceeding the Office for the Dead)

Fonds et Anches à tous les claviers. Gd. Chœur. Claviers accouplés

Jules Grison
1842–1896

160 / Grison

ten.
ten.
Tonnerre
Retirer les 32 Pieds
Moderato ♩ = 66
Récit Anches
ten.
ten.
molto ritenuto
3
Pos. (Copula Récit)
Mettre Tirasse du Récit
5
5
5
6
Pos. (Avec Récit accouplé)
G.O.
Mettre Tirasse du G.O.
un poco più animato
(Grand Choeur) con fuoco
Péd. Anches 8 P.

162 / Grison

Récit
G.O.
con bravura
rit.
con fuoco risoluto
rit.
Mettre Anches 16 P. Pédales

164 / Grison

Cloches dites Bourdons de Reims)

Quinte, Flûte et Bombarde 32 P. *ad libitum*

alla stretta

animato molto

ral - - - len - - tan - - do - - - - - **long**

Le Carillon de Saint-Paul d'Orléans

Manuale: jeux de fond 16' 8' 4'; jeux d'anches 8 et 4
    claviers accouplés.
Pédale: jeux de fond et d'anches 32, 16, 8 et 4; tirasse.

Adolphe Marty

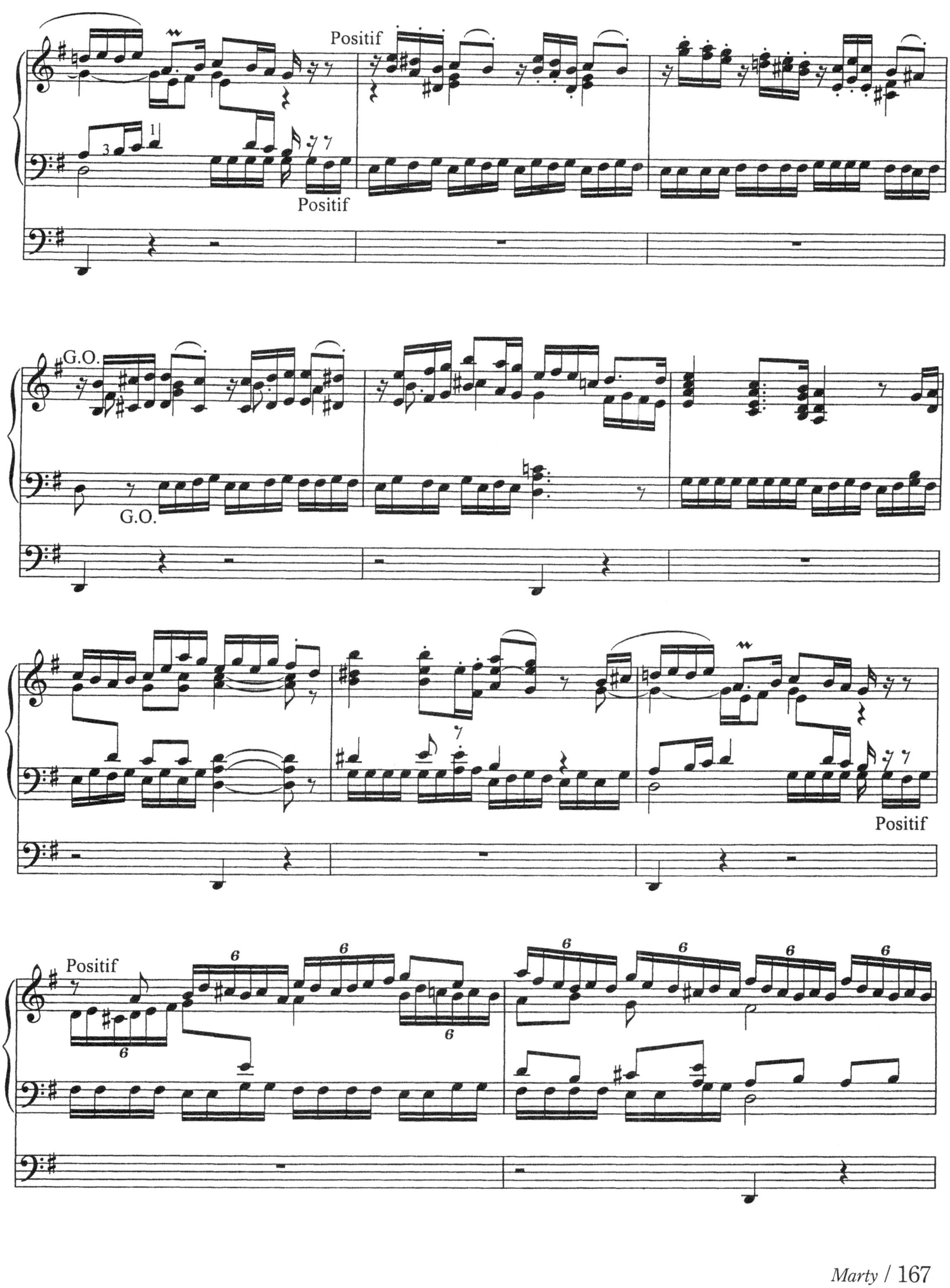
Positif
Positif
G.O.
G.O.
Positif
Positif

168 / Marty

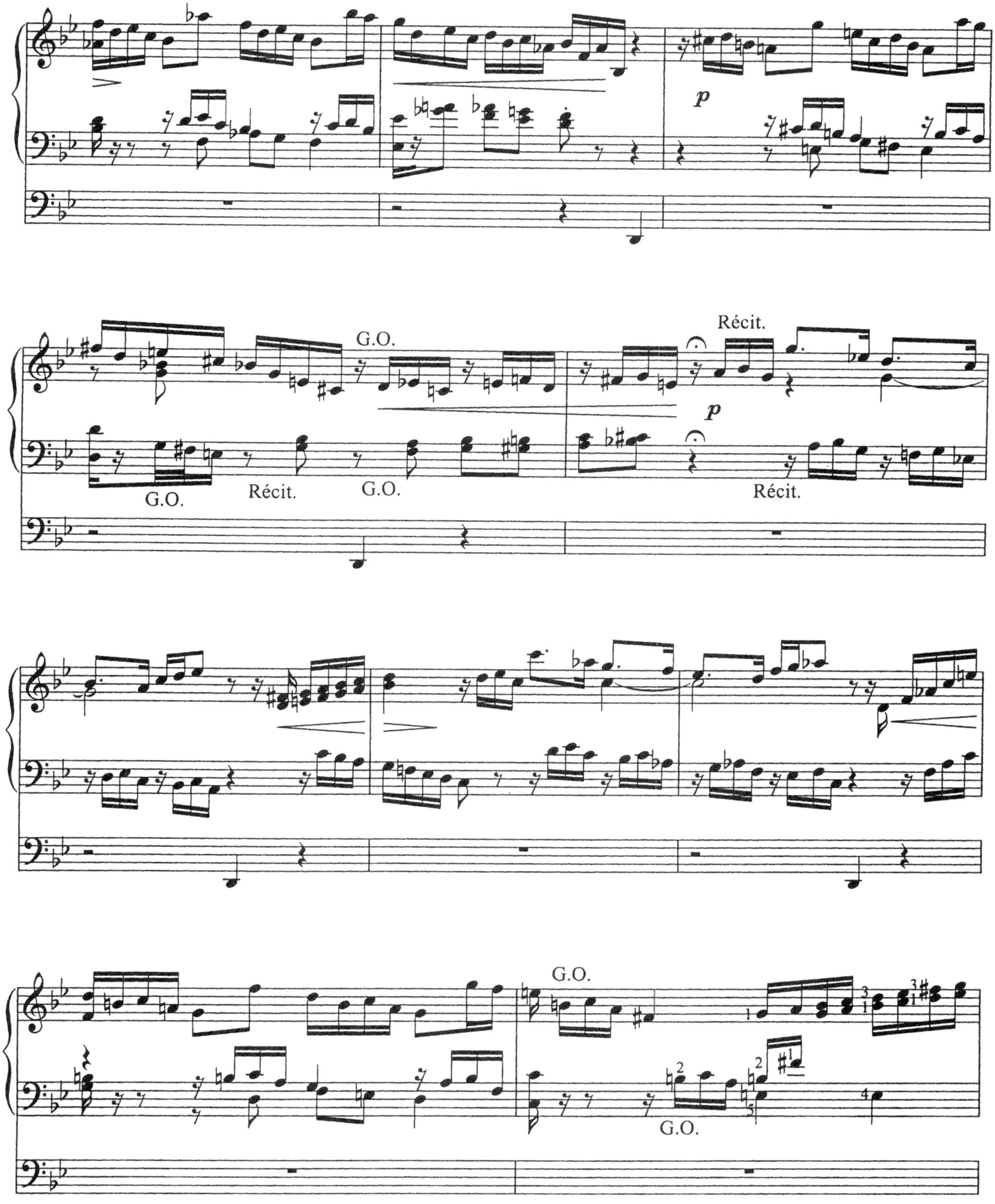
G.O.
Récit.
G.O.
Récit.
G.O.
Récit.
G.O.
G.O.

170 / Marty

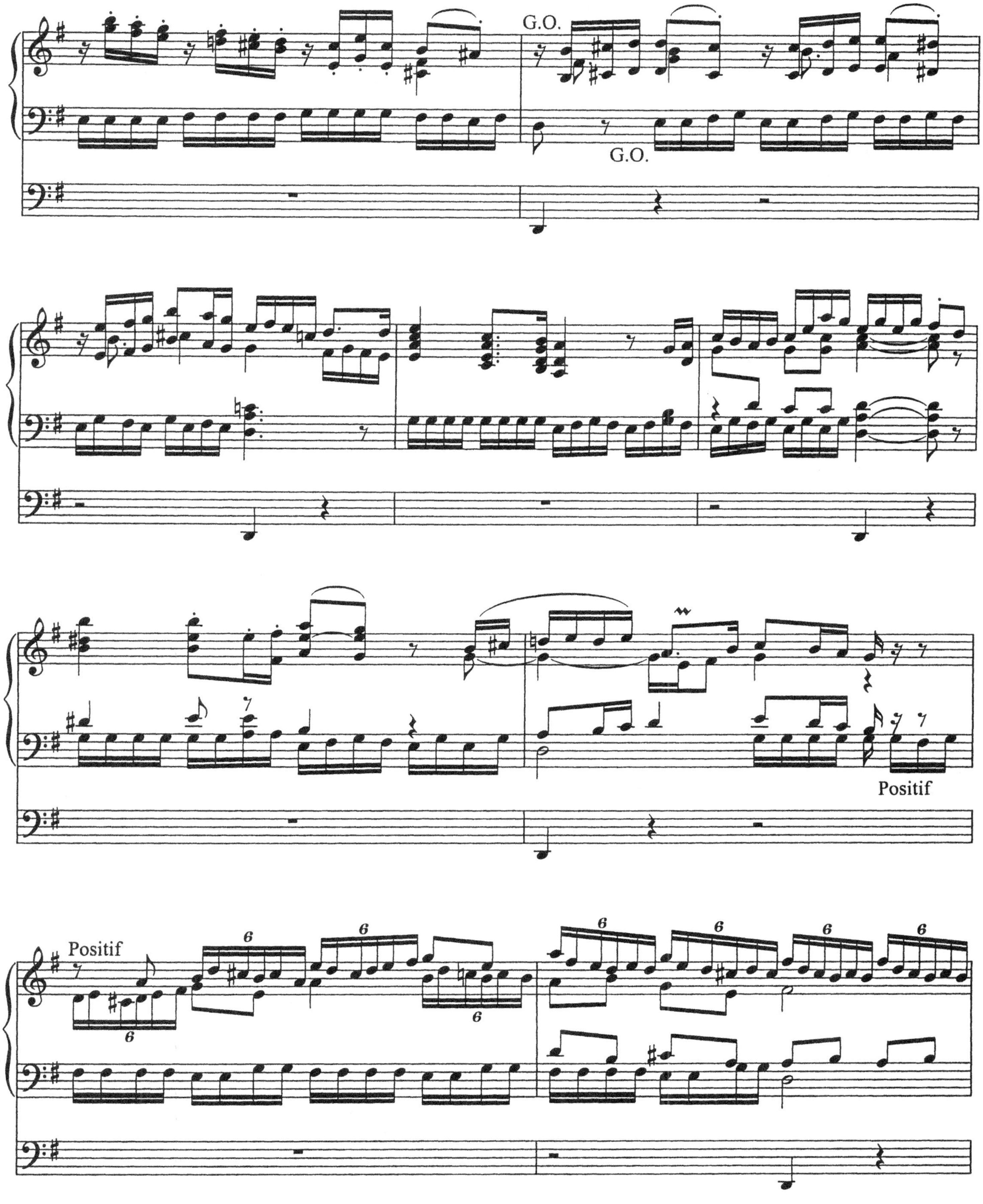
G.O.
G.O.
Positif
Positif
6

172 / Marty

RONDO
con Imitazione de' Campanelli, Op. 17

REGISTRI
Principali Bassi e Soprani
Flauti in 12 Bassi e Soprani
Ottava, Cornetta
Tromboncini Bassi e Soprani
Campanelli (*in mancanza della Vigesimanona*)

Giovanni Morandi
1777–1856

Allegro brillante

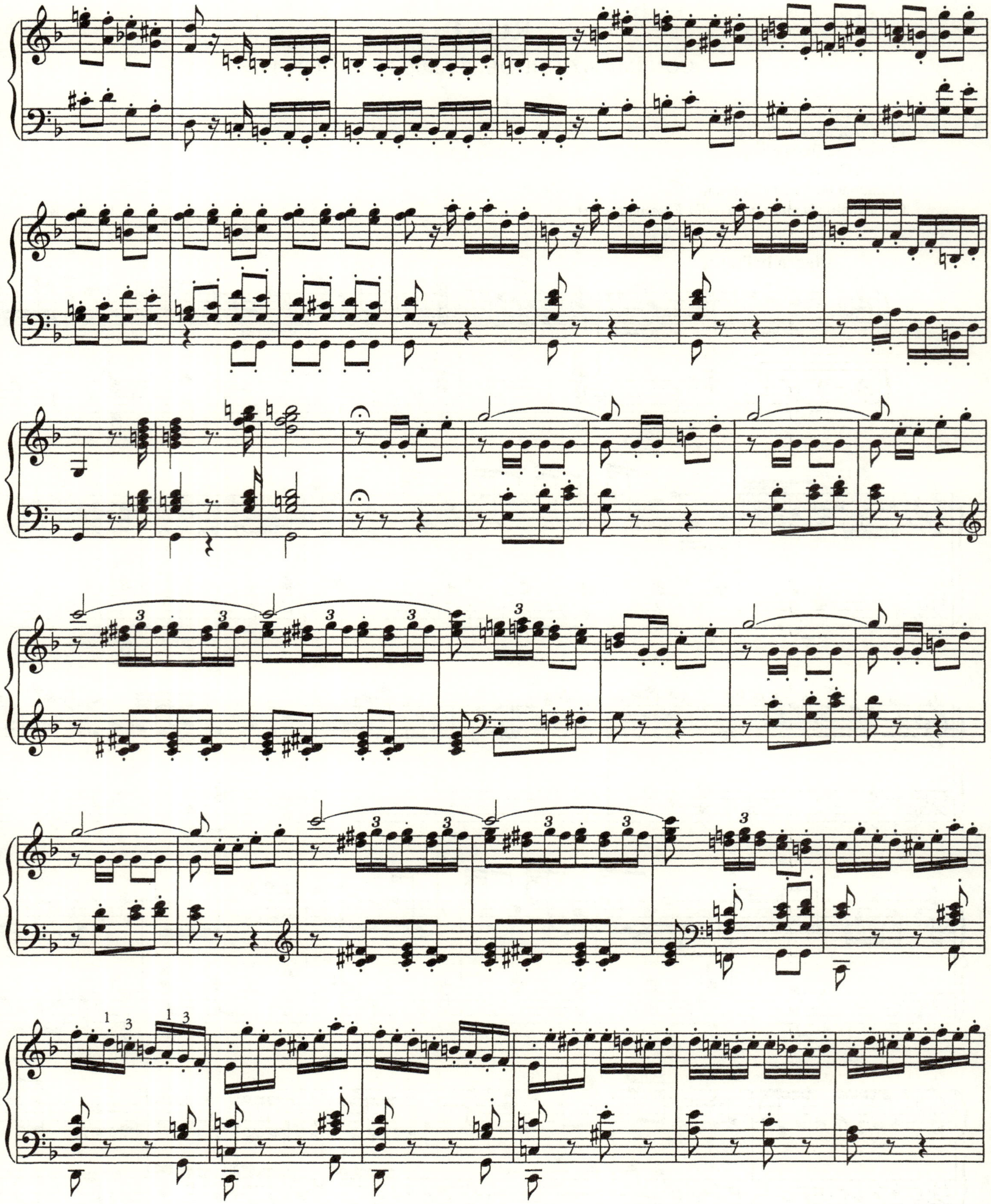
3
1

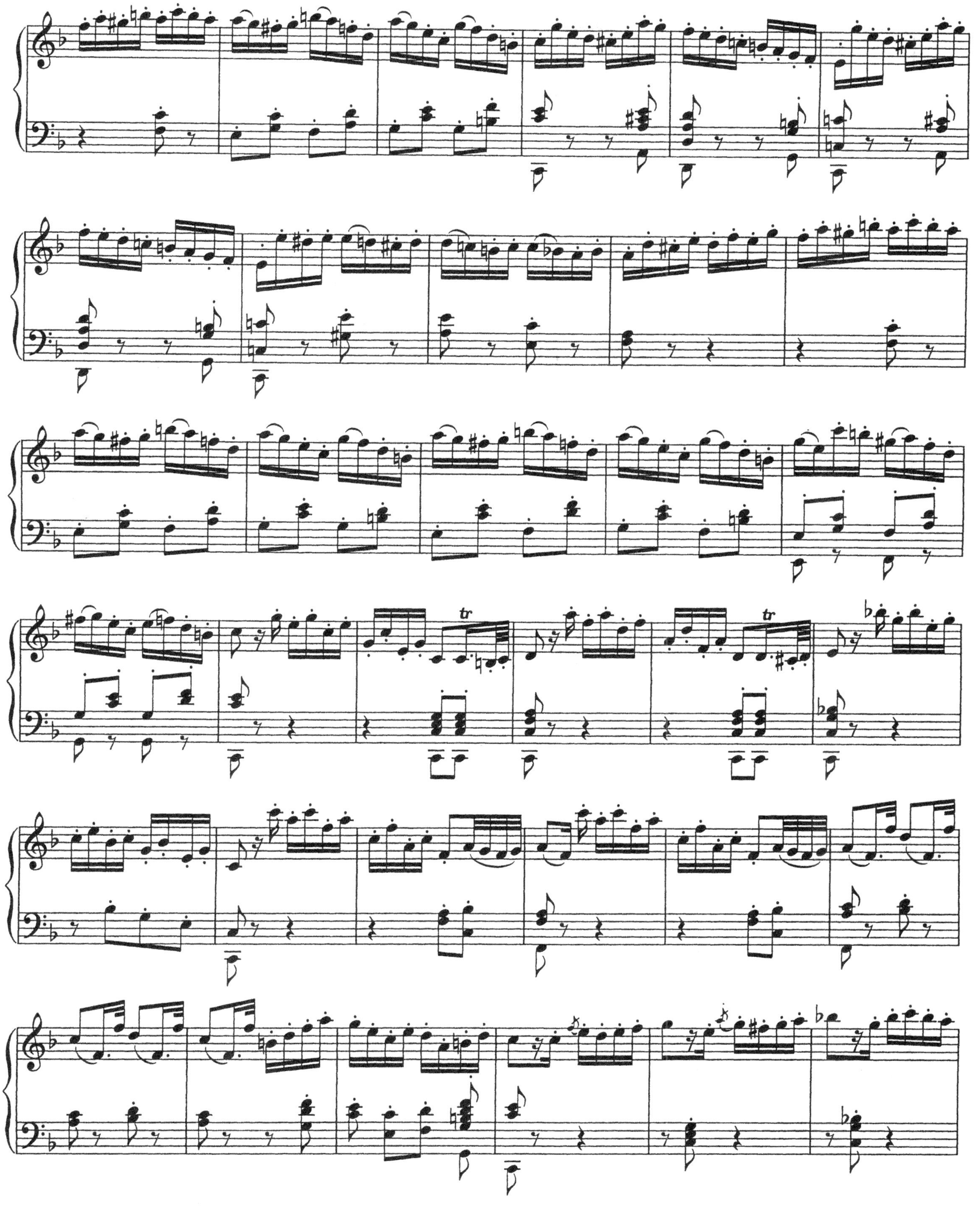
tr
tr

176 / Morandi

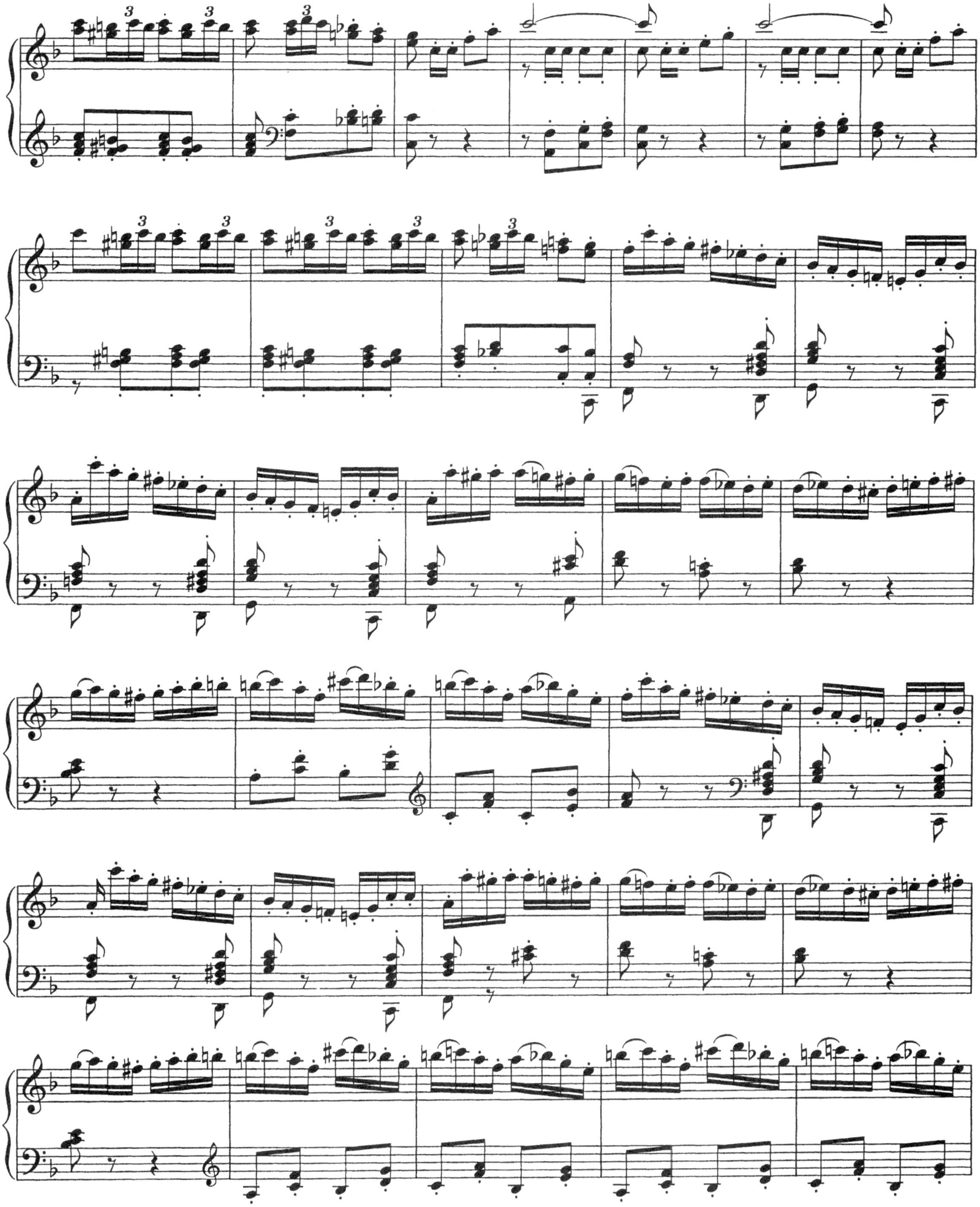
3
3
3
3
3
3
3

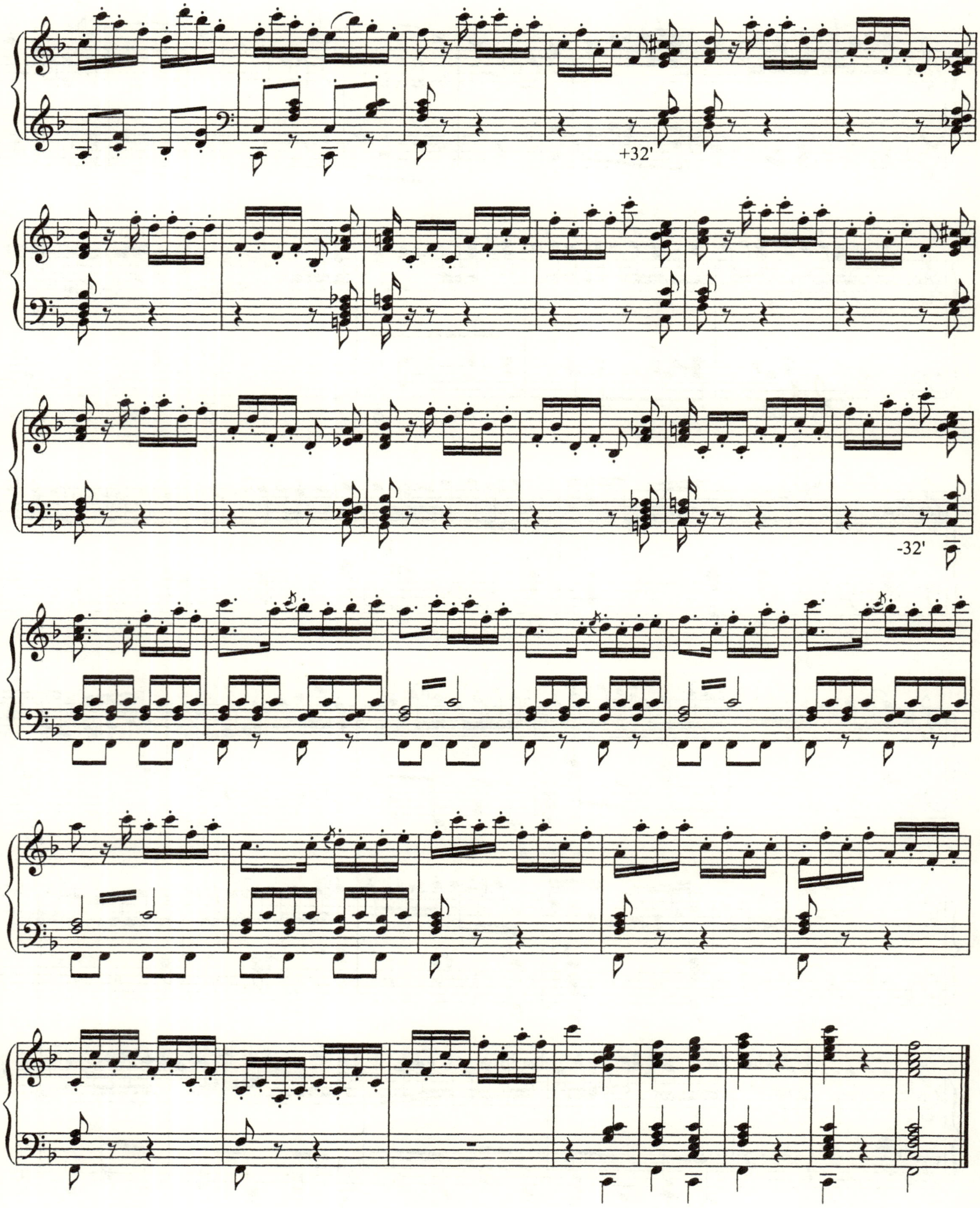
+32'
-32'

À mon ami J. Bonnet
Organiste du G.O. de Sᵗ Eustache à Paris

CARILLON - SORTIE

en Ré majeur

Indication des Jeux.
- RÉCIT: Tous les Fonds et anches.
- Gᵈ ORGUE: Tous les Fonds
- PÉDALE: Tous les Fonds

Prepare
- GT: all reeds and flues.
- SW: all flues.
- PED: all flues.

Henri Mulet
1887–1967

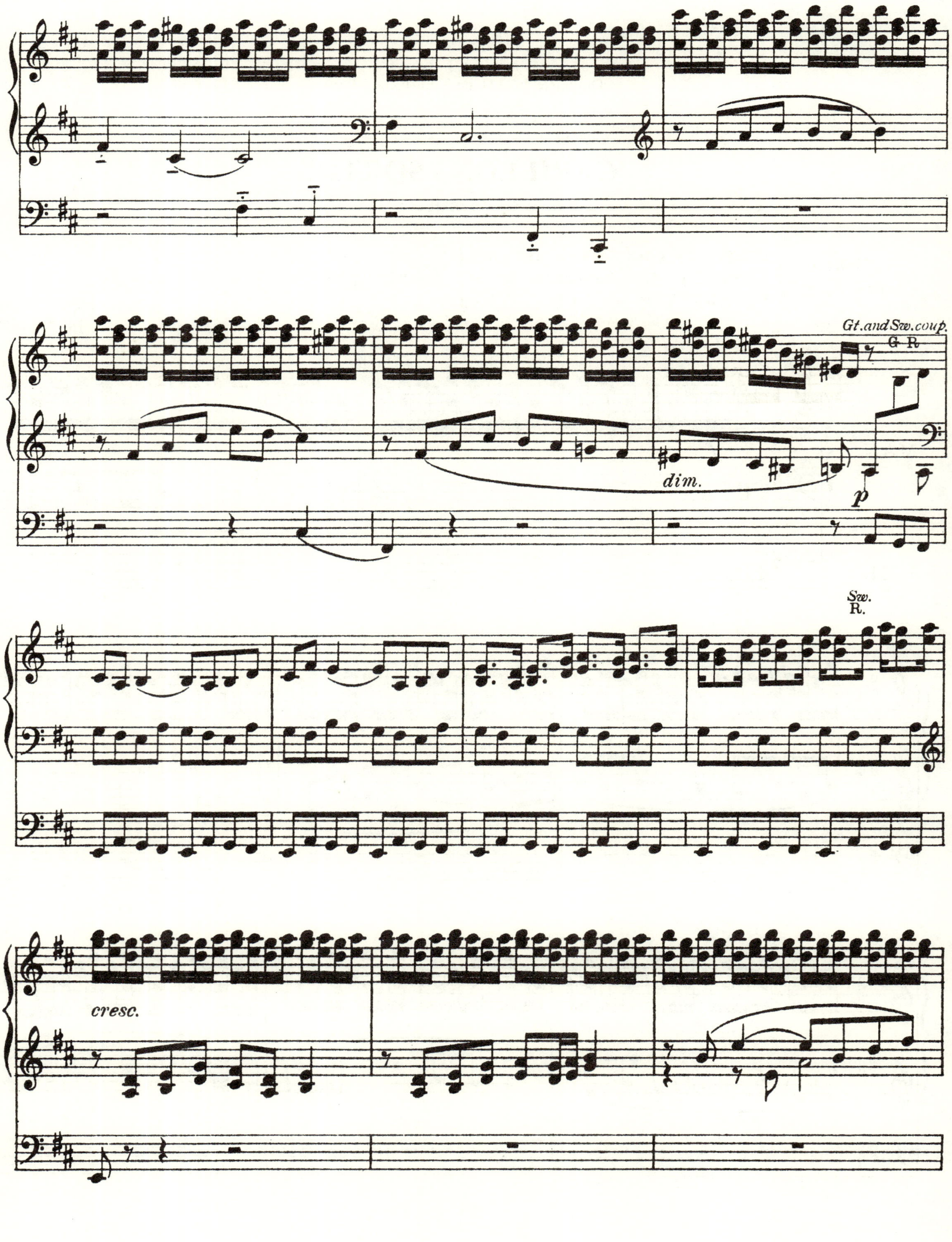
Gt. and Sw. coup.
G R
dim.
p
Sw.
R.
cresc.

Mulet / 181

182 / Mulet

Mulet / 183

184 / Mulet

Mulet / 185

186 / Mulet

Mulet / 187

188 / Mulet

For my friends, Arthur Olaf and Mary Storrs Andersen

CARILLON

Solo : Chimes (See Note 1, below)
Swell : Stopped Diap. And Voix Celeste
Great : Waldflöte
Choir : Celeste, or Harp, with 16' and 4' couplers (See Note 2, below)
       Swell to Great; Swell to Pedal
Pedal : Soft 16' and 8' stops

Leo Sowerby
1895–1968

Note 1. If the organ does not contain chimes, play the parts so designated on any suitable combination of 8' stops adding a soft 16' stop. If, however, there is a Celesta, it may be used in place of chimes, with 16' and 4' couplers and swell-box fully open.

Note 2. If the organ contains no Celesta or Harp, use instead a combination of soft flutes, 8', 4', 2', and 16'.

(increase Swell)
Sw.
mf
increase Ped.
mf
(L'istesso tempo)
(reduce Swell)
reduce Sw.
Ch.
mf
p
merrily but not too fast
Sw. Soft Flute stops 8' & 4'
Gt.
Sw.
Ch.
Ped. as before
(L'istesso tempo)

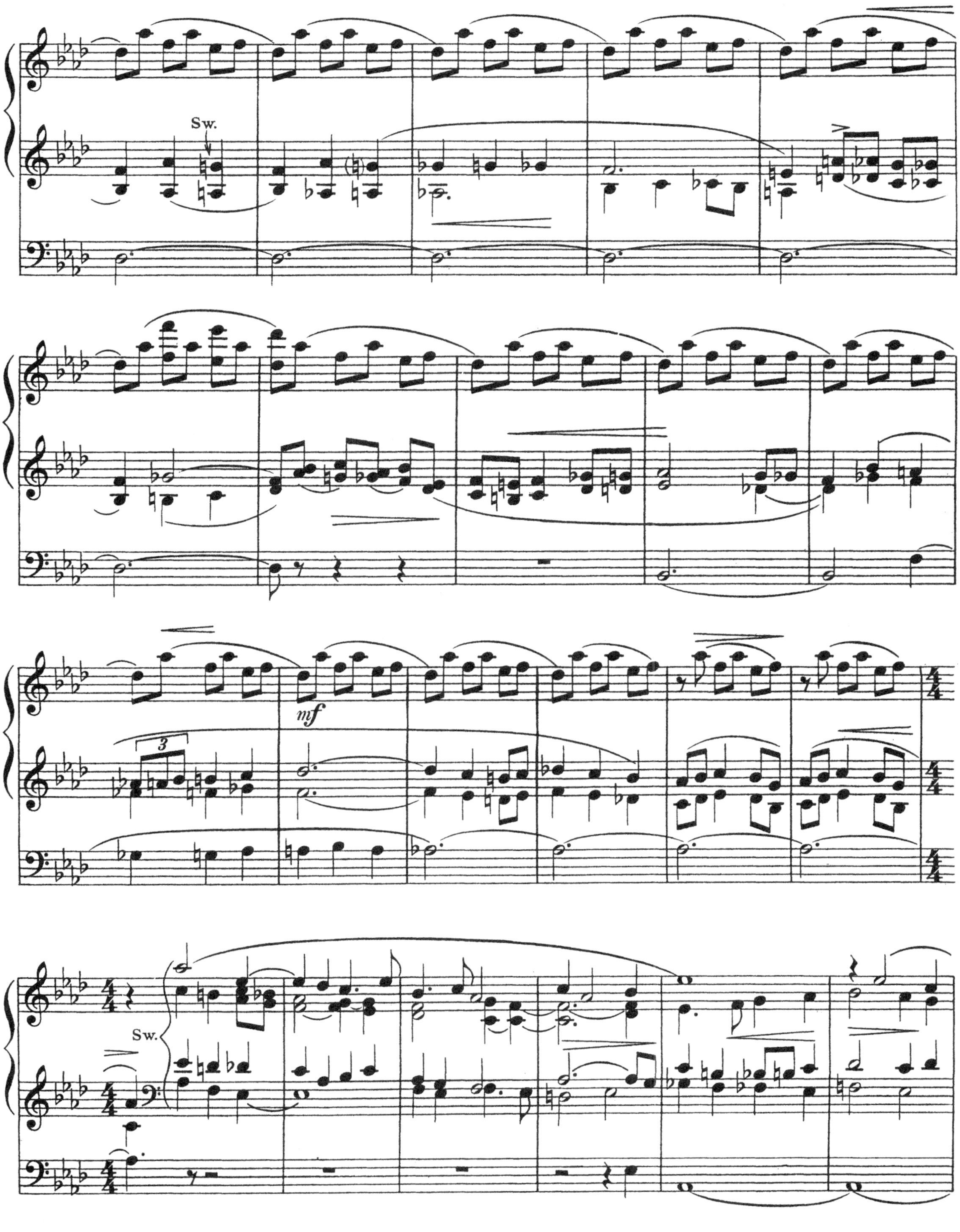
Sw.
3
mf
Sw.

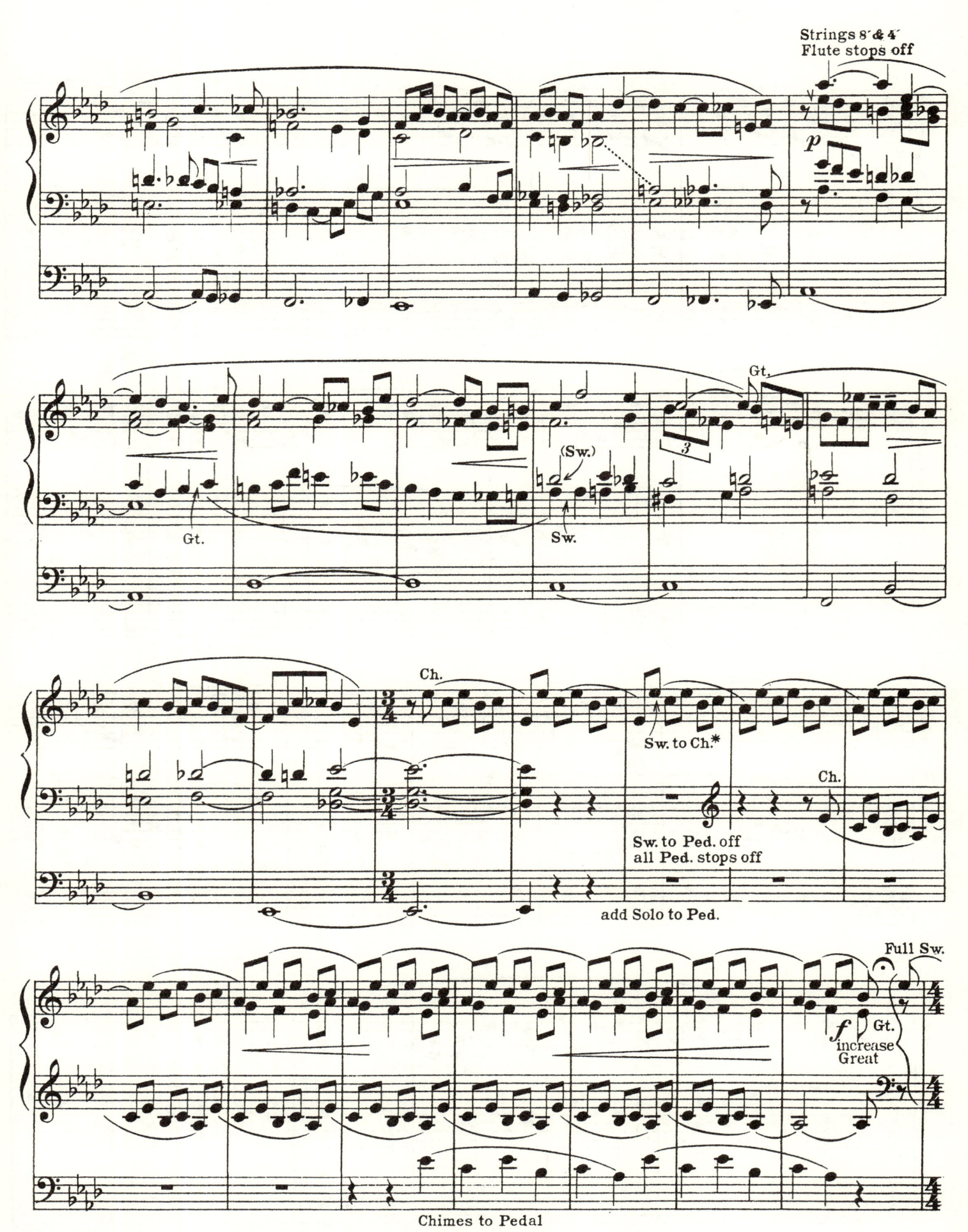

* If the Celesta on the Choir has sufficient power, do not add Sw. to Ch. coupler.

Sowerby / 193

SCHERZOS

To David McK. Williams

ROULADE
Op. 9, No. 3

Seth Bingham
1882–1972

Allegro (♩ = 124)

Bingham / 197

198 / Bingham

Prep. Gt. Diap. 8′
add Sw. to Gt.
Sw. off Reeds
Ch.
a tempo
rit.
Gt.
Gt.
f
8
Gt. to Ped.
8
(Cresc. Ped.)
full to 15th

200 / Bingham

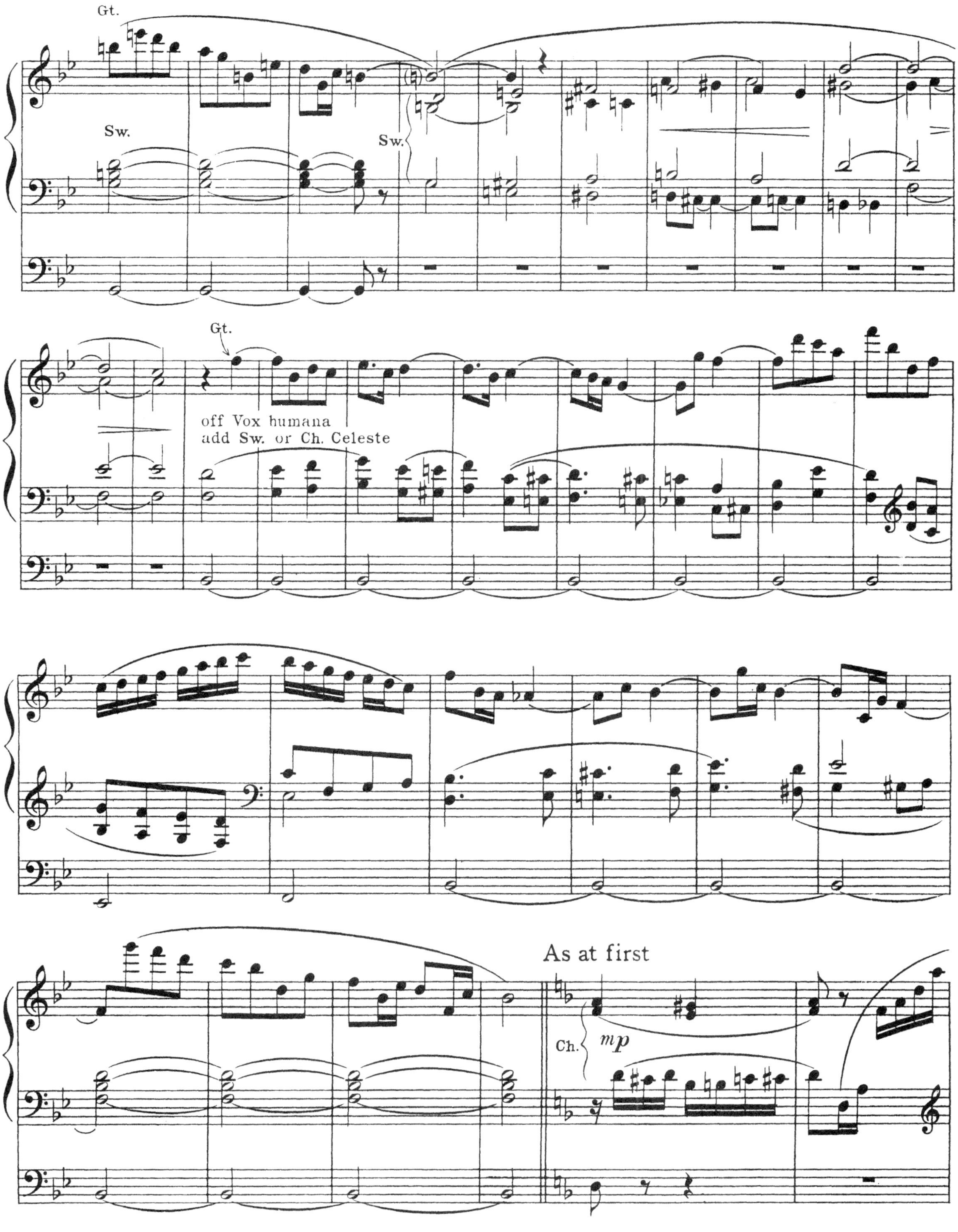
Gt.
Sw.
Sw.
Gt.
off Vox humana
add Sw. or Ch. Celeste
As at first
Ch.
mp

202 / Bingham

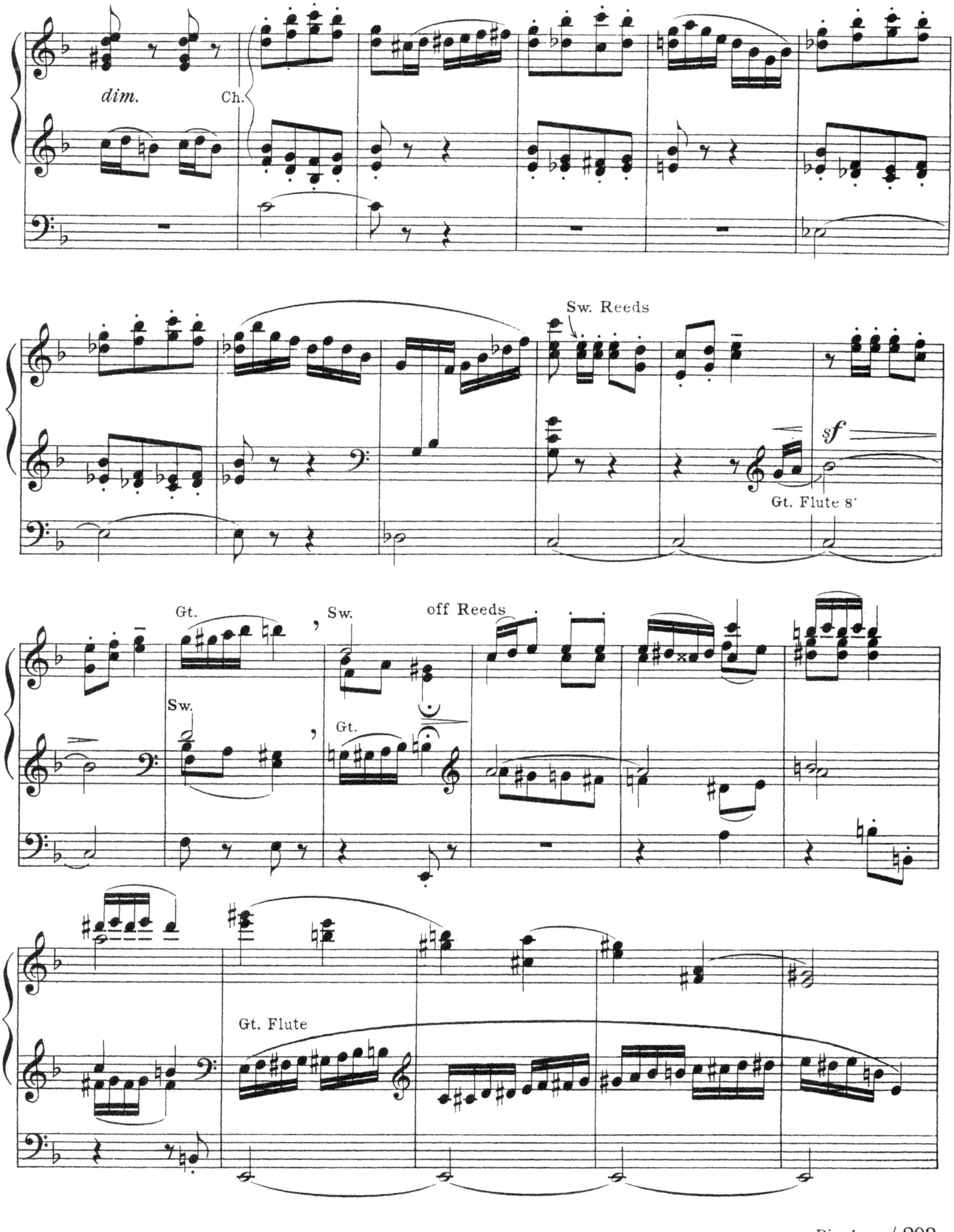
dim.
Ch.
Sw. Reeds
sf
Gt. Flute 8′
Gt.
Sw.
off Reeds
Sw.
Gt.
Gt. Flute

Sw. to Gt.
Gt.
cresc.
(Open crescendo pedal)
8
ff
(♭)
dim.
r.h.
(Reduce cresc. ped.)
8
mf
poco ten.
ff (full organ)
l.h.
(Open crescendo pedal)
poco ten.
add Reeds

Reduce, leaving Gt. or Solo Flute 8′ only in right hand
off Reeds
Ch.
f
mf
mp
Sw.
Vox humana
off Vox humana
Sw. Salicional, St. Diap. and Flute 4′
Gt. (8′ & 2′ only)

206 / Bingham

SCHERZO
in Sol Minore per Organo, Op. 49, No. 2

II. (Recitativo)   Flauti 8 e 4
I. (Grand'Organo)   8 e 4

Marco Enrico Bossi
1861–1925

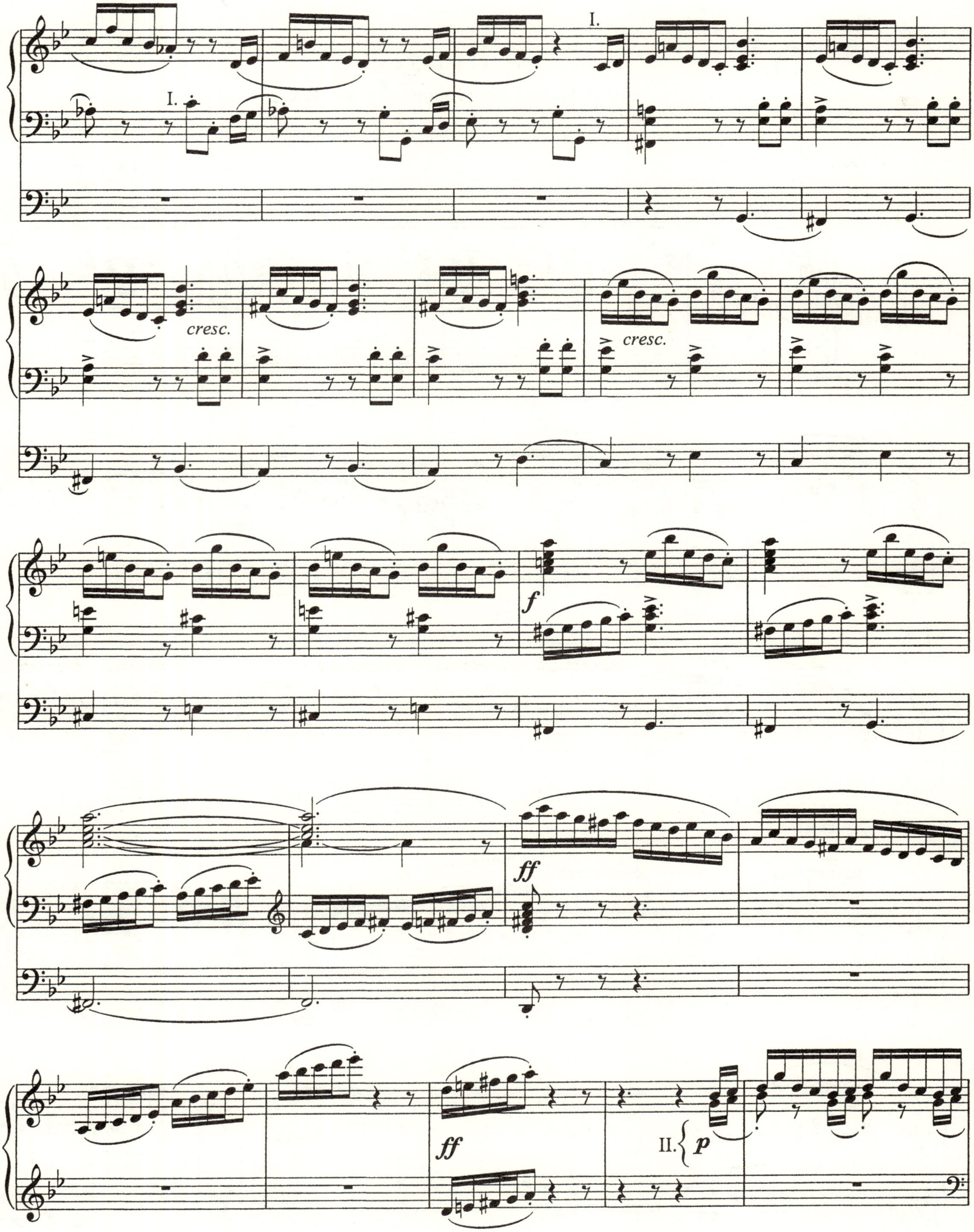
I.
I.
cresc.
cresc.
f
ff
ff
II.
p

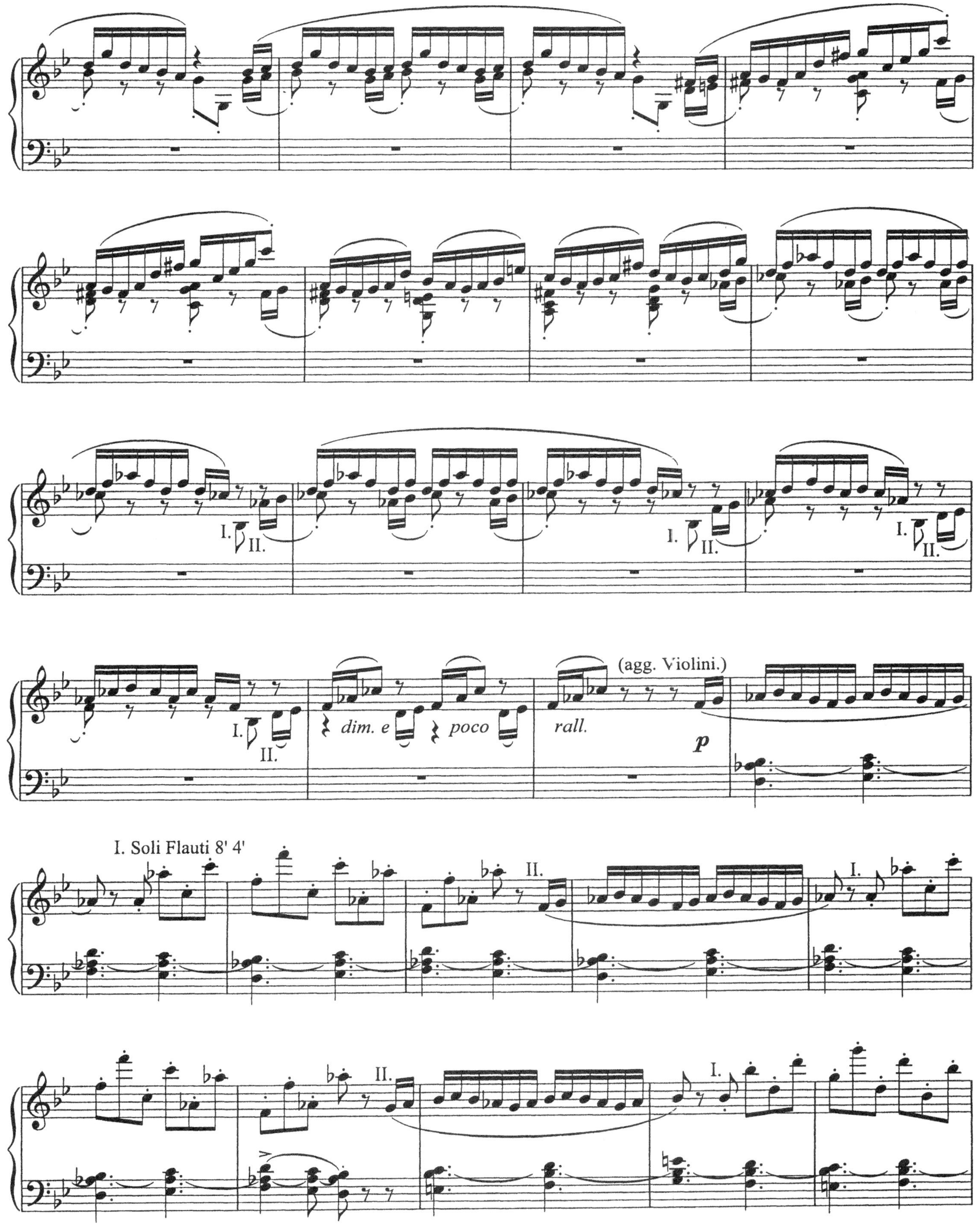

I.
II.
(agg. Violini.)
dim. e
poco
rall.
p
I. Soli Flauti 8' 4'

210 / Bossi

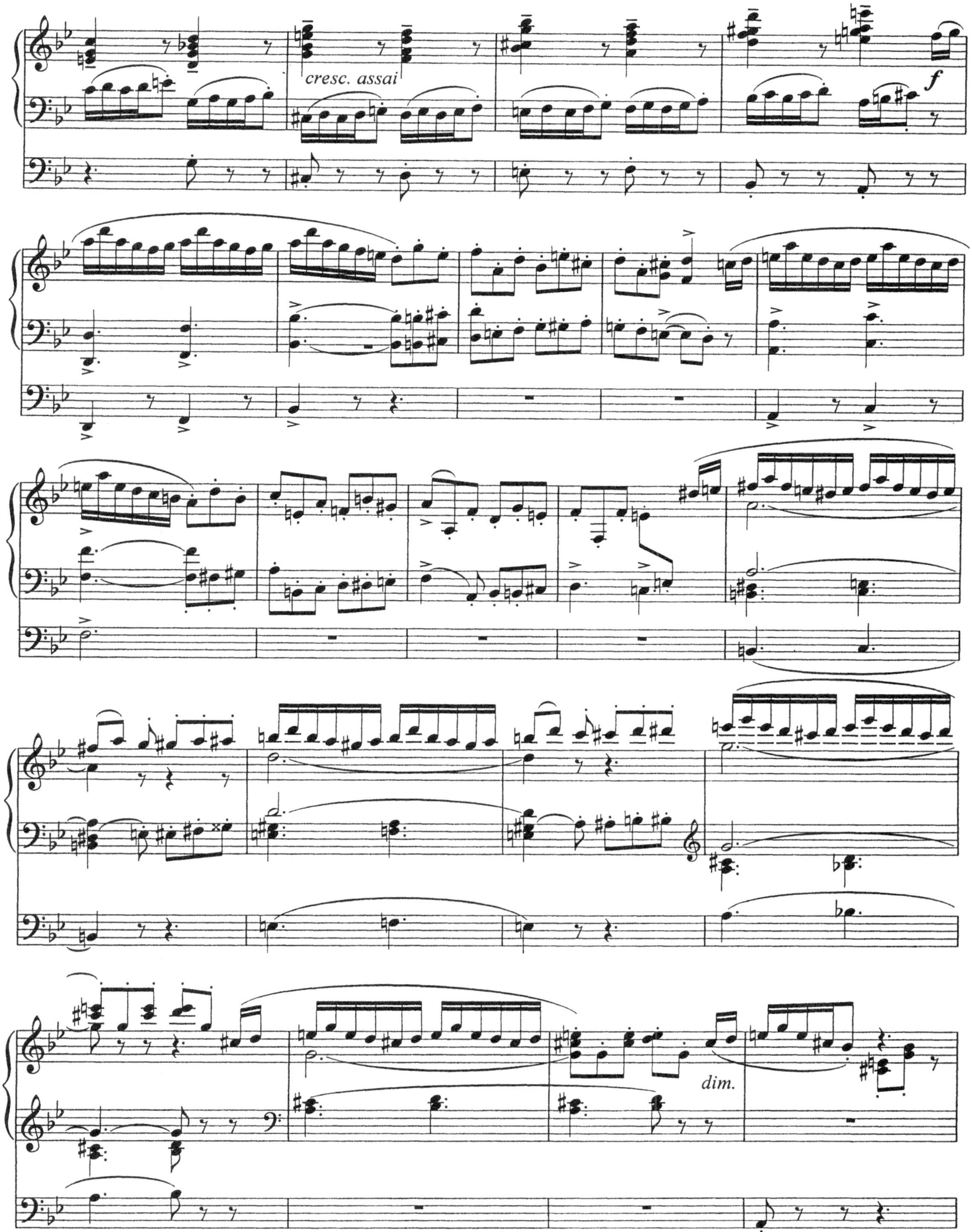
cresc. assai
f
dim.

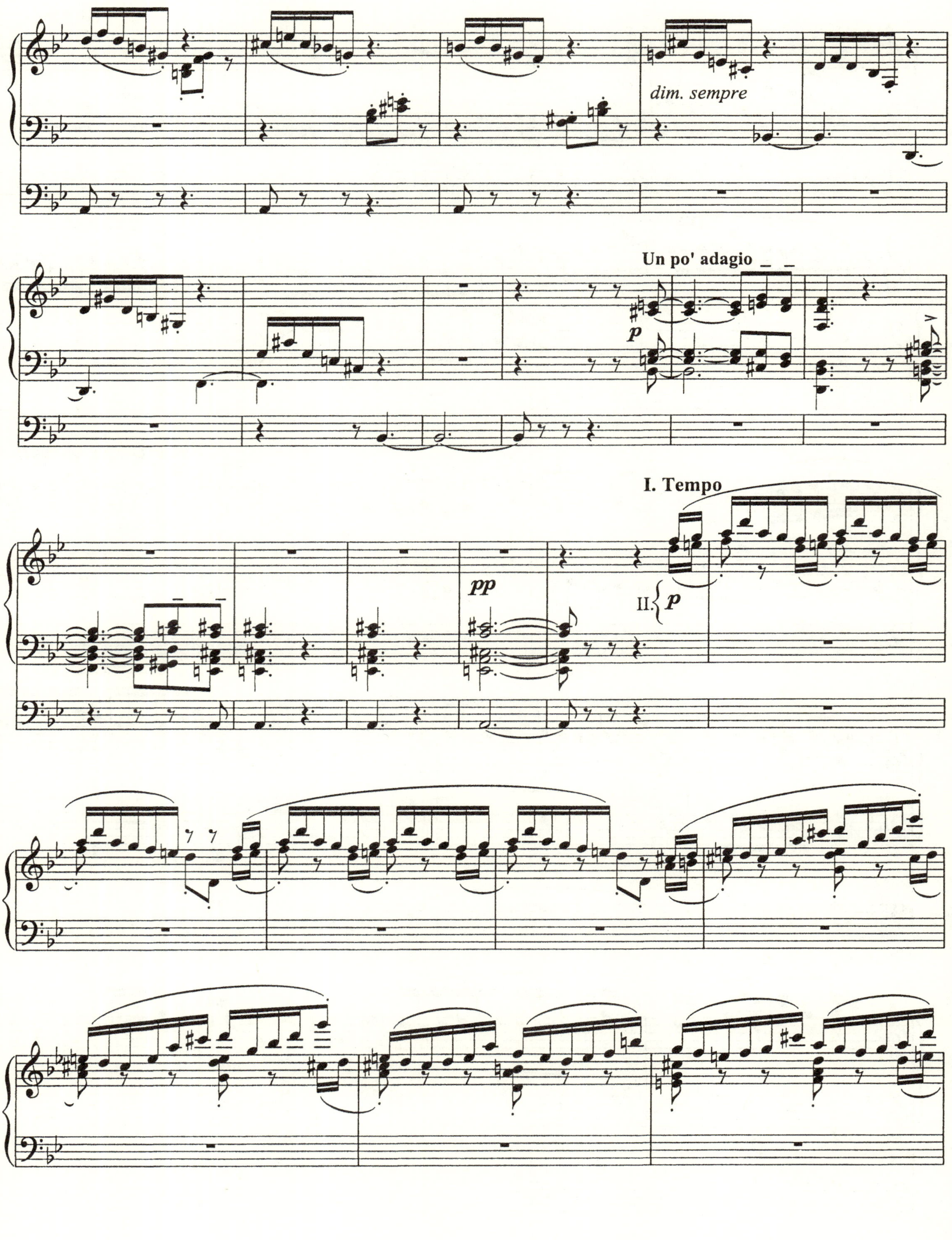
dim. sempre
Un po' adagio
p
I. Tempo
pp
II. p

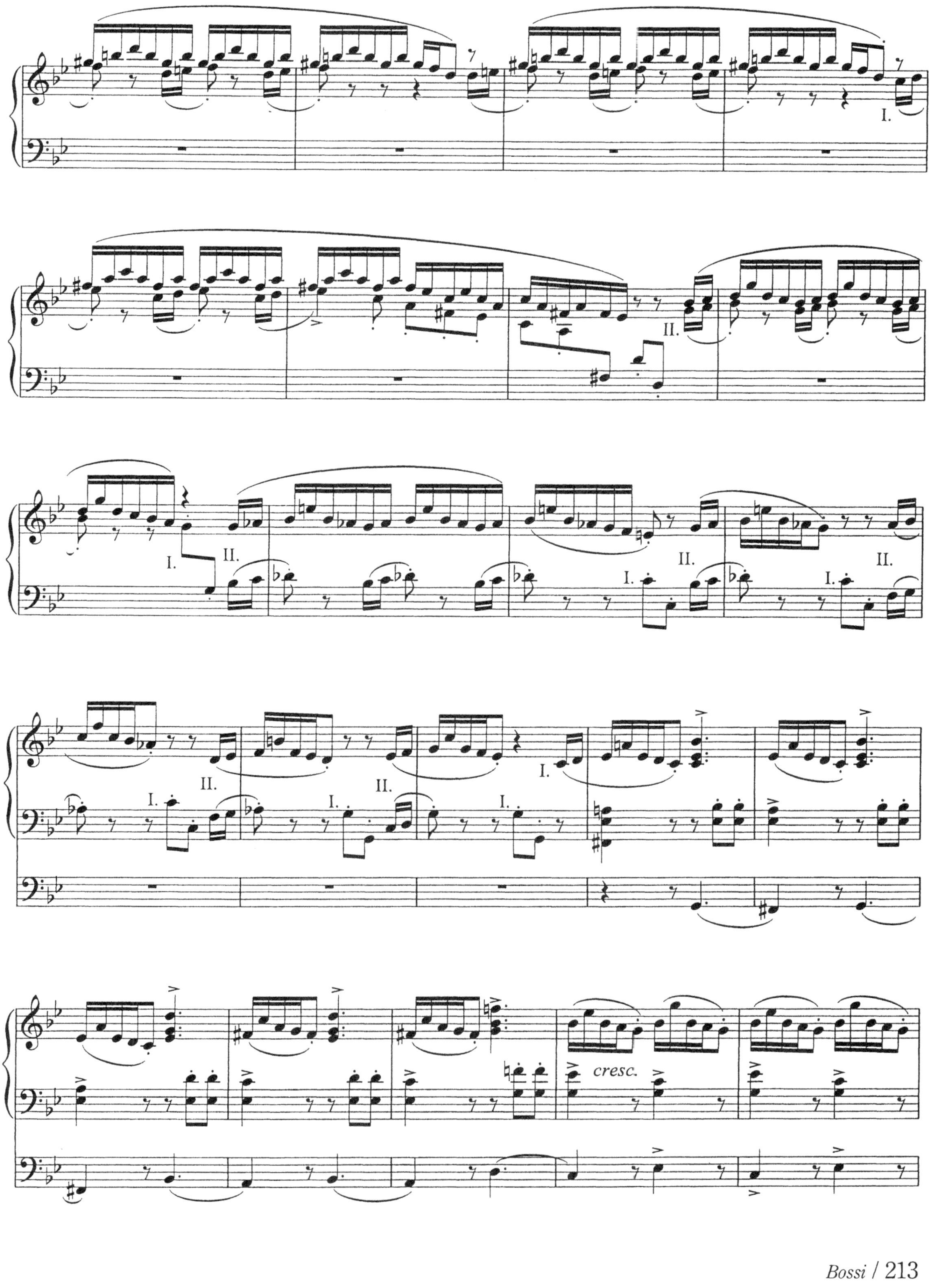
I.
II.
cresc.

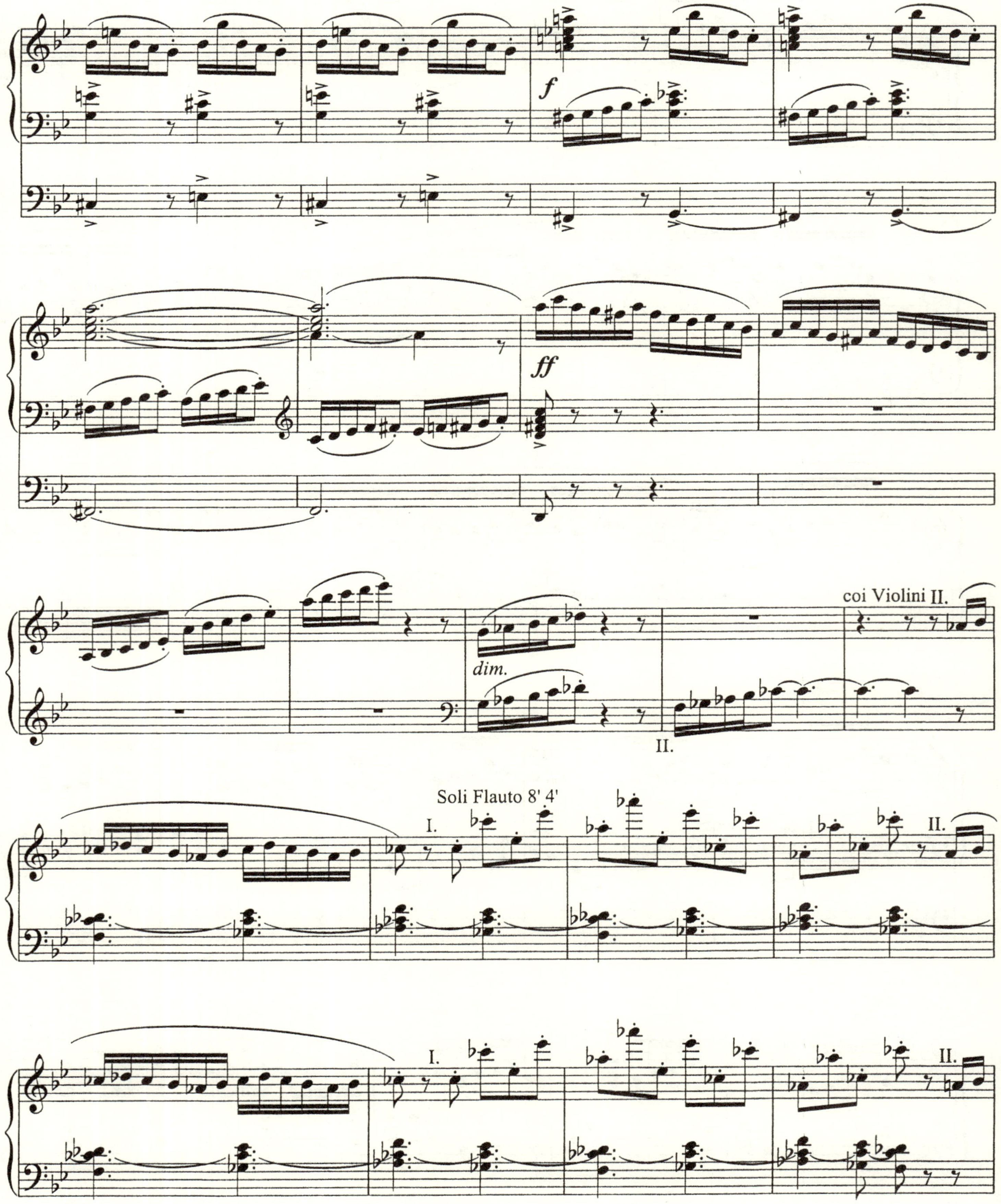
f
ff
dim.
II.
coi Violini II.
Soli Flauto 8' 4'
I.
II.
I.
II.

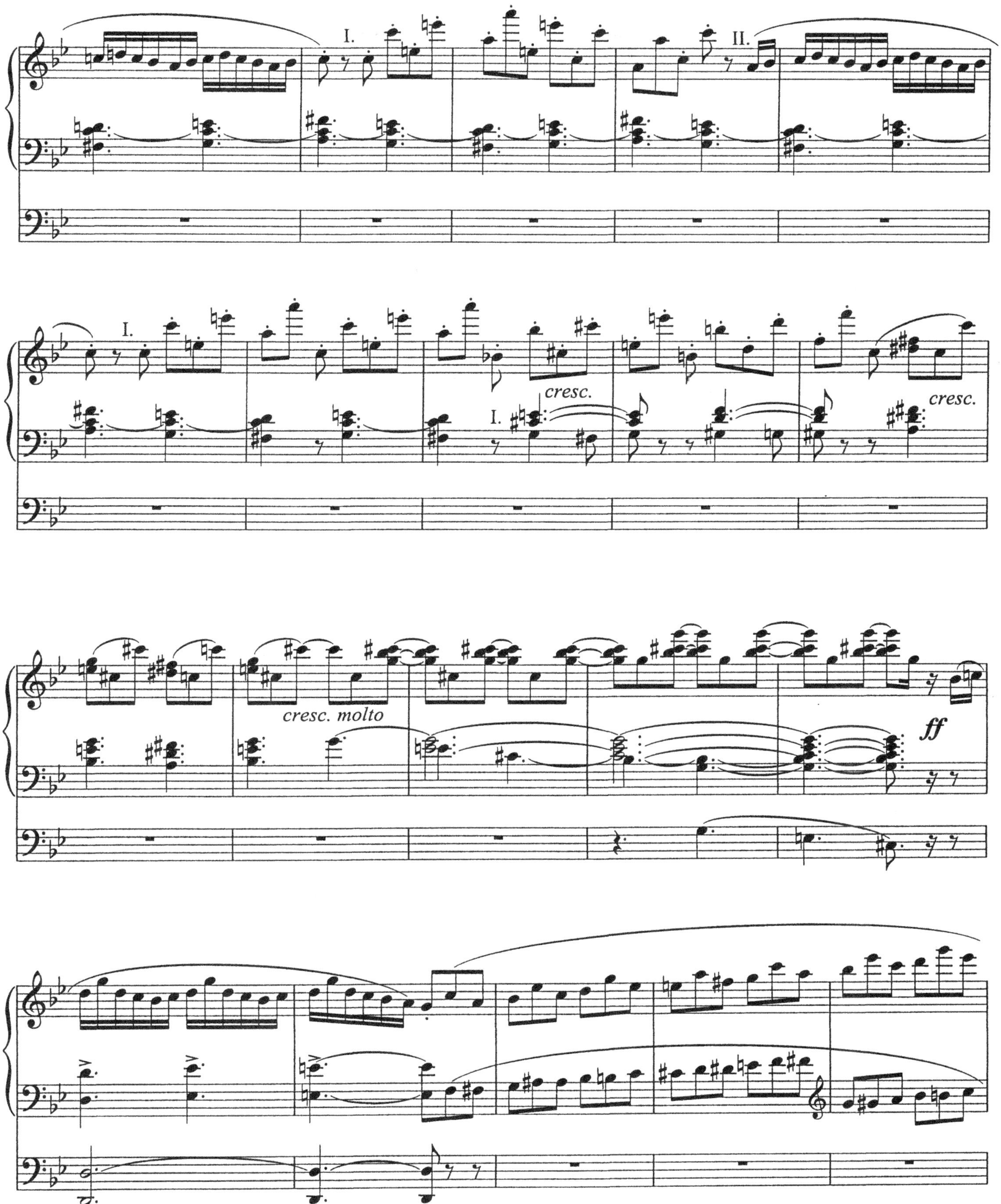
I.
II.
I.
cresc.
I.
cresc.
cresc. molto
ff

216 / *Bossi*

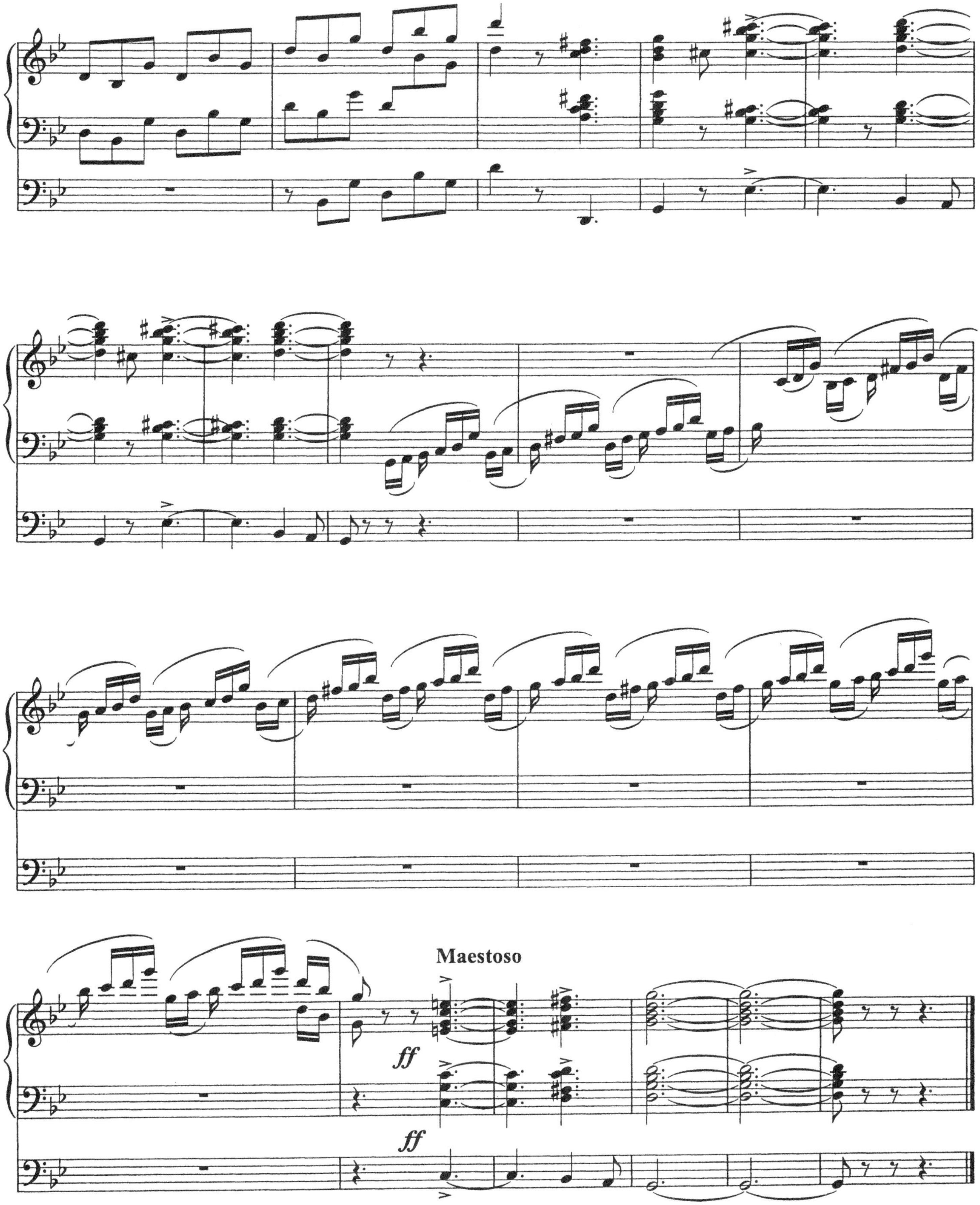
Maestoso
ff
ff

SCHERZO

Sw: Cornopean.
Gr:. Flute 8' 4'
Ch:. Principal
Ped: Bourdon 16' (Ch. to Ped.)

Gaston M. Dethier
1875–1958

Dethier / 219

220 / Dethier

CH.
p subito
legato
GR.
sfz
cresc. e accelerando
GR.
8va
f
L.H.
sfz
rit.
SW.
a Tempo
p (Vox celestis)
SW.

222 / Dethier

Add Fl. 4'
3
add 8' & 16'
16' off
cresc.
rit.
SW.
GR.
a Tempo
Oboe off.
grazioso
add 16'
8va
a Tempo
16' off
rit.
animato
a Tempo
rit.
add 16'

224 / Dethier

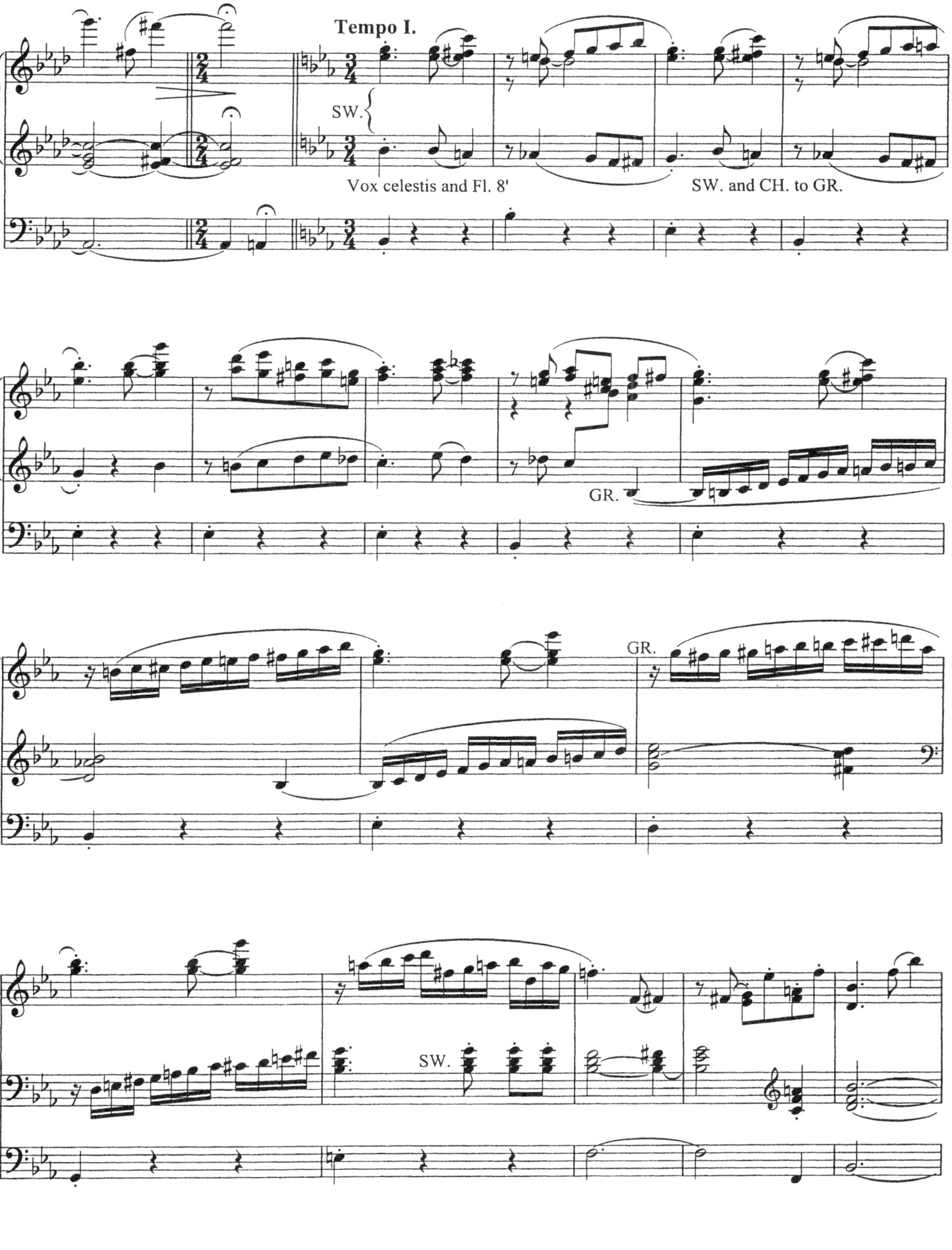
Tempo I.
SW.
Vox celestis and Fl. 8'
SW. and CH. to GR.
GR.
GR.
SW.

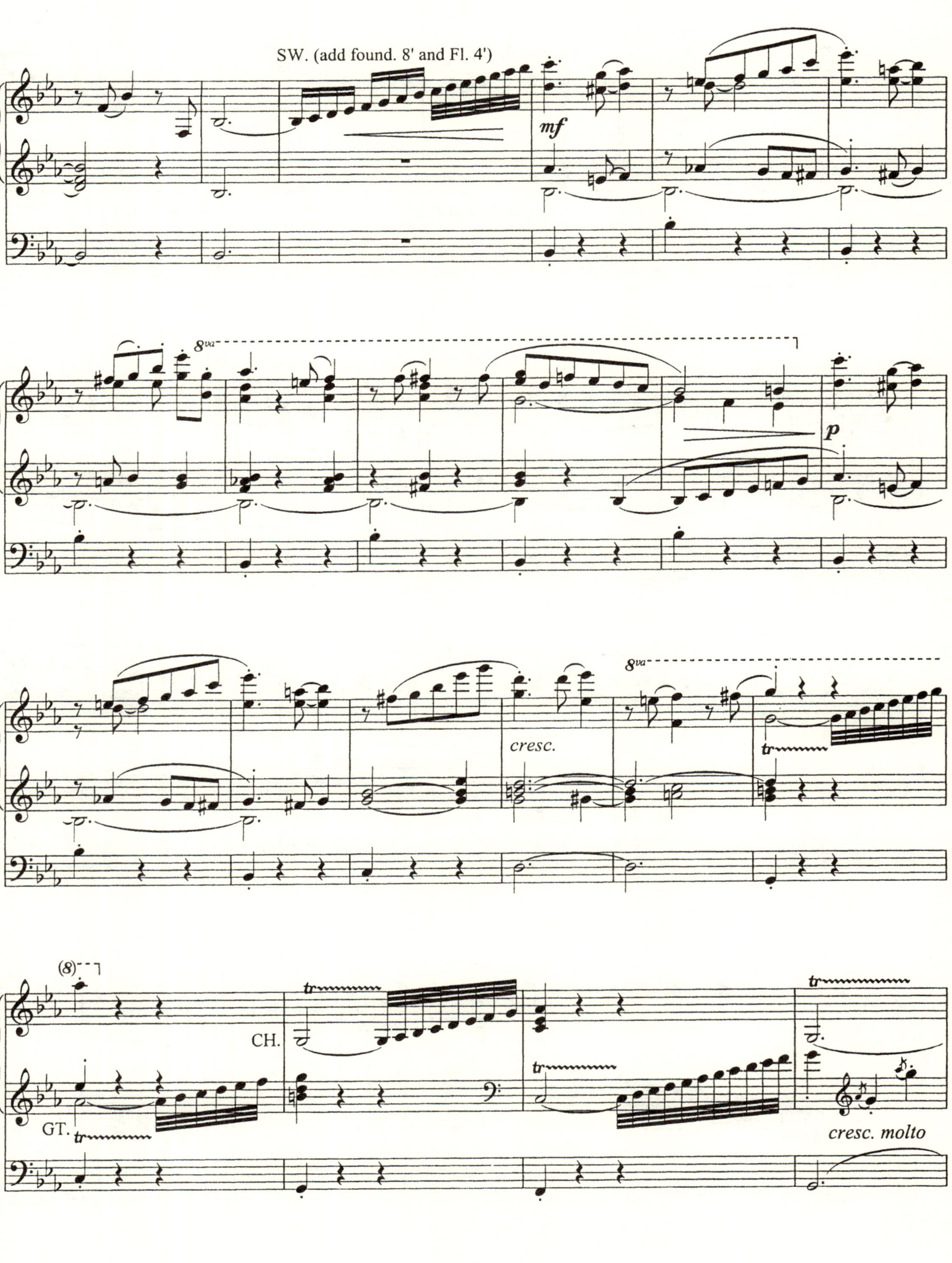
SW. (add found. 8' and Fl. 4')
mf
8va
p
8va
cresc.
(8)
CH.
GT.
cresc. molto

Dethier / 227

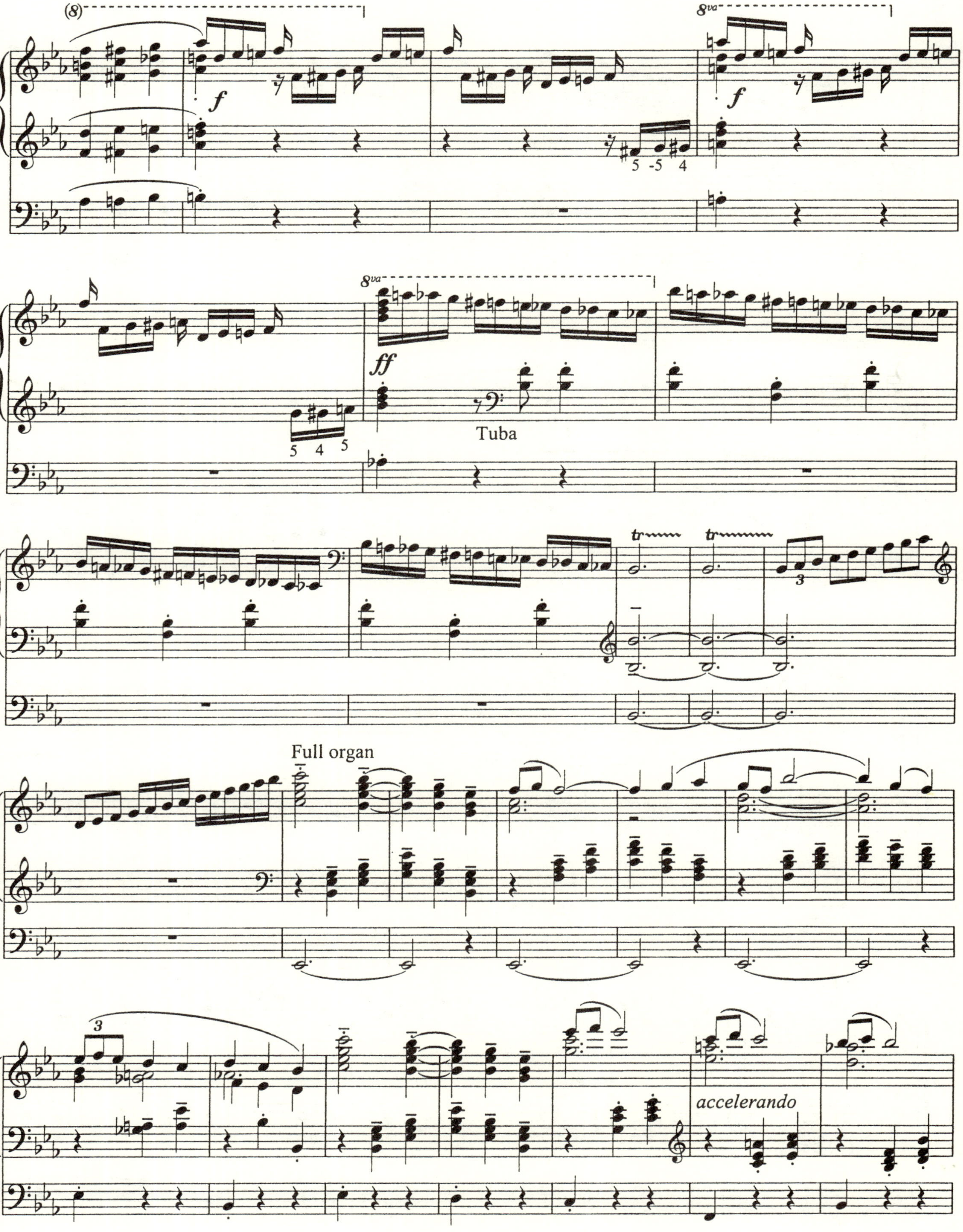

(8)
8va
f
5 -5 4
ff
Tuba
5 4 5
tr
3
Full organ
accelerando

Dethier / 229

CAPRICCIO, Op. 257
La Caccia ("The Hunt")

Polibio Fumagalli
1830–1900

Fumigalli / 231

232 / Fumigalli

Fumigalli / 233

234 / *Fumigalli*

sf
f
sf
f
affrettòsosino alla fine
f
sf
sf
f
f
f
affrettòso
dim.
p
ritard. assai
p

À *Monsieur* M.J. ERB

SCHERZO

Récit. Fonds et Anches de 8 et 4 p.
G^d Orgue. Fonds de 8 et 4 p.
Pédale. Fonds de 16, 8 et 4 p.

Eugène Gigout
1844–1925

Gigout / 237

238 / Gigout

Gigout / 239

240 / Gigout

Gigout / 241

242 / Gigout

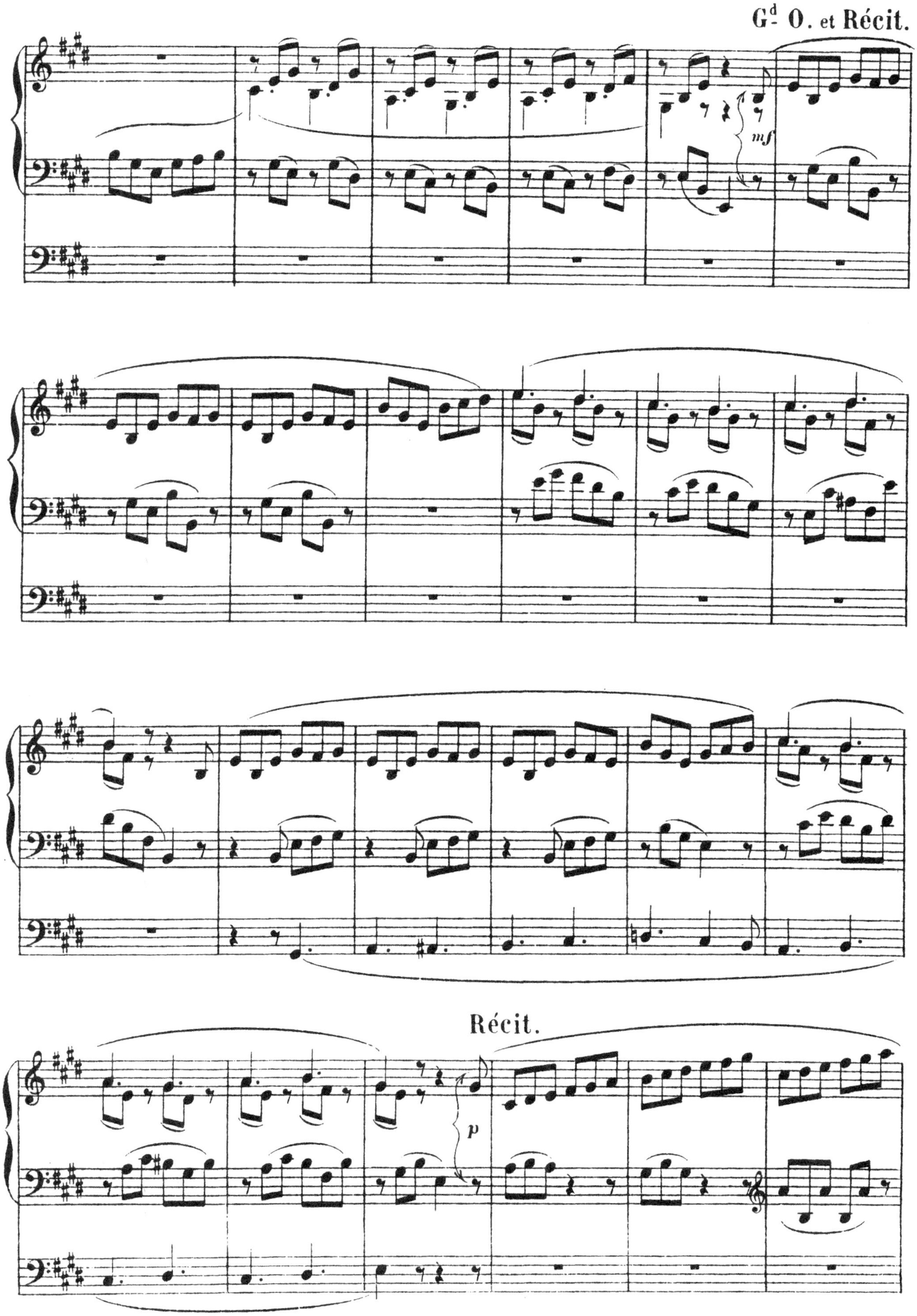
Gd O. et Récit.
mf
Récit.
p

Gᵈ O. et Récit.

(Boîte ouverte)
f

244 / Gigout

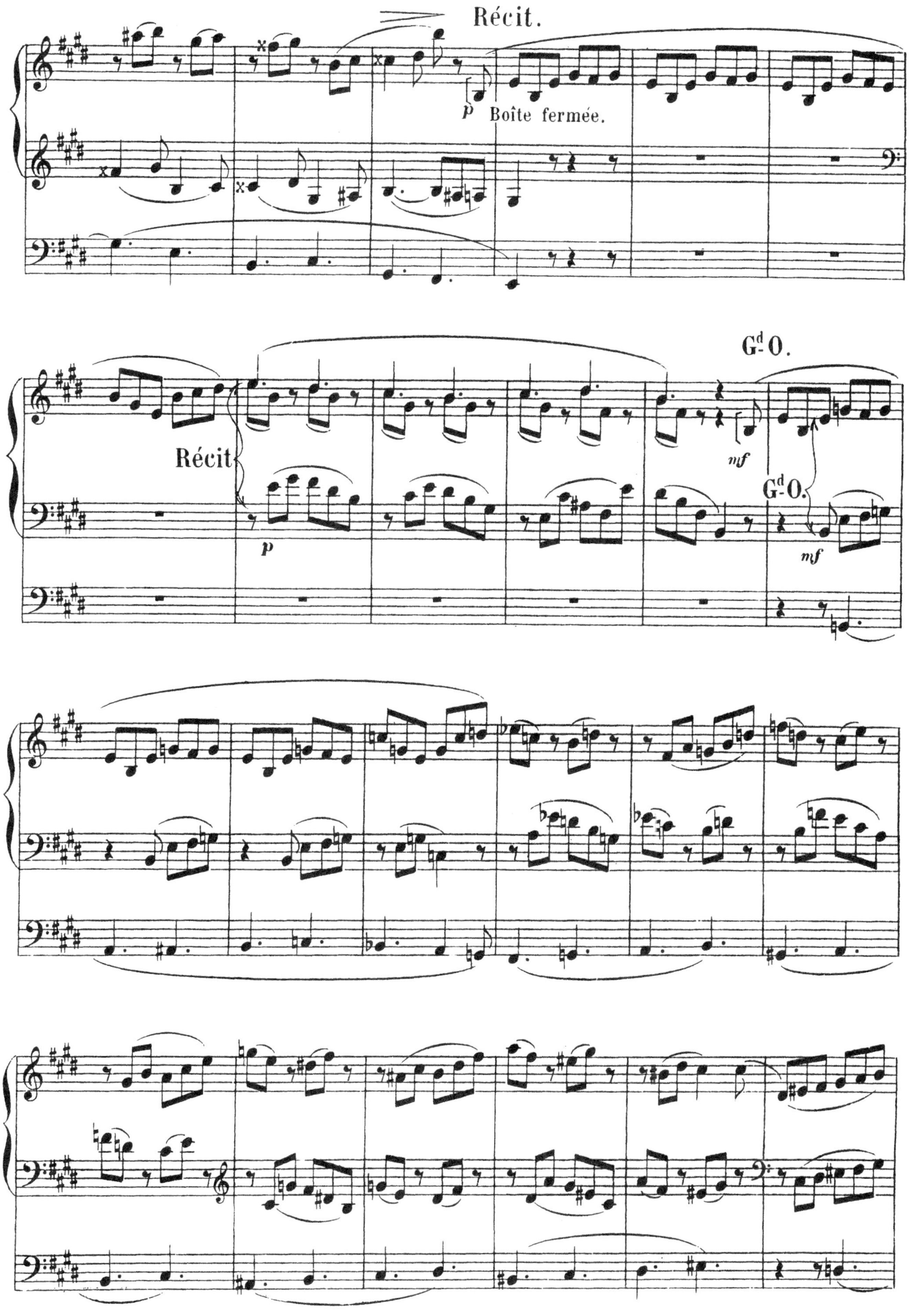
Récit.
p
Boîte fermée.
Récit
p
Gd O.
mf
Gd O.
mf

Cre - - scen - - do.
f
Boîte ouverte.
Sempre f
Récit
Gd-O.
Récit
Gd-O.
R.
Boîte fermée.
p